# WORLD CUP
## PLAYER BY PLAYER

# WORLD CUP
## PLAYER BY PLAYER

First published in the UK in 2014

© G2 Entertainment Limited 2014

www.G2ent.co.uk

Printed and bound in Europe

ISBN 978-1-782812-30-2

# CONTENTS

# Introduction

Enamoured with the success of the amateur Olympic football tournaments in the 1920s, Jules Rimet, a French football administrator and the third President of FIFA, pressed the organisation to found the World Cup. Uruguay were unofficial World Champions as they had won the 1924 and 1928 Olympics so the country was chosen to host the first tournament in 1930, which coincided with the centenary of its independence.

Brazil was expected to do well at the event but it was local rivals Argentina and the hosts who would make it to the final, with Uruguay winning the trophy named in Rimet's honour. Four years later the football world descended on Italy and the hosts would win again, but the tournament was weakened by having only one South American side (Brazil) make the long and expensive trip to Europe. In 1938 the tournament was staged in France. Brazil were now a force on the world stage and striker Leônidas was one of the stars of the event. He scored four goals against Poland in a thrilling 6-5 win, although Wilimowski also netted four times for their opponents. Brazil lost to Italy in the semi-final but then beat Sweden in the playoff to claim third place.

The Second World War robbed many players of their best years but in 1950 the tournament was held in Brazil for the first time. The public expected much from their side and they didn't disappoint, initially at least, with centre forward Ademir embodying all that was good about South American football.

England entered this World Cup for the first time believing that as champions of the old world and indeed the old style they would have no problem bringing the trophy home. But England were dumped out by the USA in one of the biggest sporting upsets of all time, while the flair and skill of the Brazilians took the game to a different level. They thrashed Olympic champions Sweden 7-1 in the new Maracanã Stadium in front of nearly 200,000 people and then smashed six past Spain to claim their place in the de facto final (the latter stages of this tournament were played in a round-robin format and Brazil only needed a draw against neighbours Uruguay to win their first World Cup).

The game seemed to be going to plan when Friaça put Brazil ahead, but Schiaffino equalised for Uruguay midway through the second half. Eleven minutes from time, Ghiggia broke through the Brazilian defence and beat Barbosa at the near post. Brazil had somehow snatched defeat from the jaws of victory, and the country went into mourning.

In 1954, the magnificent Magyars of Ferenc Puskás were tipped to lift the Jules Rimet Trophy in Switzerland as they had been unbeaten since 1950. Brazil came up against this formidable team in Bern in one of the most violent matches ever played. Hungary won but three players were sent off and the fighting continued amongst the players in the tunnel afterwards as well as the fans and stewards on the pitch. Hungary were then expected to win the final against West Germany as they'd hammered them 8-3 earlier in the tournament but the Germans took advantage of poor conditions to grind out a famous victory.

Two years later Brazil came to England for the first time to play a friendly at Wembley. The old world was finally meeting the new. Brazil were 2-0 down to the hosts within four minutes, but Paulinho rifled in a low shot from a tight angle just after the break and then Didi equalised. Tommy Taylor put England back in front with a close-range header, and then Gilmar

saved two penalties. Stanley Matthews provided a cross for Granger to head home late on and give England a 4-2 victory. It was obvious to most, however, that Brazilian skill and pace would soon outclass English muscle and determination.

By 1958 Brazil had toughened up physically without sacrificing any of the flair, and a 17-year-old Pelé scored a deflected goal in the World Cup quarter-final against Wales to set up a meeting with France in the semi. Vavá opened the scoring but the incomparable Just Fontaine equalised before Didi restored a slender lead for the South Americans. Pelé then stole the show with a tap in, a close-range shot with the outside of his right foot, and finally a powerful right-foot shot into the bottom corner to make it 5-2. They won the final by the same score although they went behind to a brilliant solo goal from Nils Liedholm. Vavá equalised from a few

**Above:** *One of the first England squads*

yards and then scored an identical goal to put Brazil 2-1 up. Pelé scored a magical goal after 55 minutes by flicking the ball over the defender's head and finishing into the bottom corner. Zagallo then poked the ball home to make it 4-1 but Sweden pulled one back through Simonsson. Pelé scored again with a header in the last minute, however. It was Brazil's first World Cup victory and planet football rocked to a samba beat.

Pelé scored a magnificent solo goal in Brazil's opening match at the 1962 World Cup in Chile but he then picked up an injury. Brazil avenged their Wembley defeat by knocking England out of the tournament in the quarter-final. In the semi they overcame the hosts to set up a meeting with Czechoslovakia. The Czechs took the lead through the incomparable Josef Masopust but Brazil equalised through Pelé's replacement Amarildo, and he then provided the cross for Zito to give Brazil

the lead. Vavá pounced on a mistake from the Czech goalkeeper to seal the victory and back-to-back World Cups.

In 1964 Alf Ramsay's England toured Brazil to mark the 50th anniversary of their football association. Brazil took the lead in the anniversary match but Jimmy Greaves equalised in the second half. Pelé then set Ronaldo up for his second before scoring his first and Brazil's third. He turned provider again shortly afterwards as Brazil scored their fourth. They added a fifth in the last minute and looked certain to lift the Jules Rimet Trophy for the third time at the next World Cup in England in 1966. England had learned from their mistakes, however, and with Bobby Charlton marshalling the midfield they brushed aside the competition before winning an epic final against a West Germany side boasting the likes of Uwe Seeler and Franz Beckenbauer. When Geoff Hurst rifled the ball into the top corner in the last minute of extra time he became the first – and so far only – man to score a hat-trick in the World Cup final.

Pelé was constantly fouled throughout the tournament and vowed not to play in another World Cup. Having scored his 1,000th goal in 1969, and with new coach and former team-mate Mário Zagallo now at the helm of the national team, however, he changed his mind and joined the side in Mexico in 1970. Brazil went a goal down in their opening match against the Czechs but Rivelino equalised with a thunderbolt free-kick and Pelé then gave Brazil the lead before Jairzinho added another two. Jairzinho then scored the winner against England in a match of such quality that it was dubbed 'The final that never was'. It was also memorable for Gordon Banks's wonder save from a Pelé header. Brazil had to overcome a stern challenge from Uruguay in the semi-final but they then brushed Italy aside in the final (4-1). This was the beautiful game at its finest, the zenith of Brazilian football.

Brazil were a spent force in the 1970s and the balance of power shifted perceptibly towards the Dutch with their interchangeable total football and the Germans with their characteristic determination and clinical finishing. The two sides met in the final of the 1974 World Cup and the Dutch scored a penalty before their archrivals had touched the ball. The German's fought back through the outstanding Gerd Müller and went on to win 2-1.

The Netherlands reached consecutive finals when they came up against hosts Argentina in 1978. It had been a controversial tournament because Argentina needed to beat Peru by four or more goals to progress to the final at unbeaten Brazil's expense. Peru were a decent side so their 6-0 defeat has never been satisfactorily explained. Mario Kempes proved the difference in the final itself, his two goals consigning the Netherlands to defeat after extra time.

Brazil were expected to do well in 1982 as a new golden generation of players like Zico, Sócrates, Júnior and Falcão were now in their prime. In their first match against the USSR, the Soviet Union took the lead but Sócrates and Éder scored wonderful long-range efforts to seal the win. They also went behind against Scotland but Zico, Oscar, Éder and Falcão then scored to give them a comfortable win. They came unstuck against a Paolo Rossi-inspired Italy in a pulsating game that was eventually decided by some poor defending. Rossi had been pilloried for his performances in the group games because he had been out of the side for two years after a conviction for match-fixing and clearly wasn't fit. He then came good, however, scoring a wonderful hat-trick against Brazil and another goal in the final against West Germany.

Argentina's Diego Maradona dominated the 1986 World Cup. In a tense quarter-final against England he scored one of the most controversial goals in World Cup history when he leaped above Peter Shilton and punched the ball into the net. His second goal in the match was the polar opposite, however. He beat half the English team with a mazy dribble from inside his own half and then rounded Shilton to poke the ball home. It was perhaps the greatest individual goal ever scored.

Brazil showed flashes of brilliance – such as Josimar's two wonder goals – but they ran into Platini's France in a quarter-final of intoxicating brilliance. Careca opened the scoring but France equalised through Platini. Then Branco was brought down in the box and Zico stepped up to take the penalty but it was saved by Joël Bats. The keeper also saved Sócrates's spot-kick in the subsequent shootout, but Brazil were thrown a lifeline when Platini put his penalty into orbit. Júlio César then hit the post and Fernandez won the game for France with a cool strike into the bottom corner. The French were then beaten by a West German side destined to mirror the consecutive World Cup final defeats of the Dutch. Maradona may have been a marked man in the final but he still provided the killer pass for Jorge Burruchaga to apply the coup de grace.

Despite Maradona being past his best in 1990, Argentina still made it to the final. The tournament in Italy had been poor, however, with many teams employing defensive tactics and hoping they got lucky in the resulting penalty shootouts. Franz Beckenbauer's Germany were the exception and their positive attitude and offensive formation saw them overcome a negative Argentina in a dour final.

By 1994 Brazil finally boasted some of the best players in the world and in Romário and Bebeto they had the most feared strikers. Goals from Romário and Raí helped them overcome Russia and then they cruised past Cameroon, but they could only draw with Sweden. A late Bebeto goal saw them edge past hosts USA in the first knockout round, and more goals from Romário, Bebeto and Branco were enough to beat the Netherlands in the quarter-final. Romário was on target once more in the semi against Sweden and Brazil won their fourth World Cup with victory over Italy in a penalty shootout after a poor game.

Brazil made the final four years later at France '98 after wins over Scotland, Morocco, Chile, Denmark and the Netherlands. In the build-up to the match against the hosts, however, Ronaldo suffered a suspected seizure and the team

**Above:** *The best team in history, the Brazilian World Cup squad in 1970*

was off its game in the final. The French had already beaten South Africa, Saudi Arabia, Denmark, Paraguay, Italy and Croatia so they were a formidable outfit anyway. Two Zidane headers and a late Petit goal gave France victory but Brazil would bounce back in style four years later in Japan and South Korea. With a fit Ronaldo, Brazil won their group with three wins, saw off the challenge from Belgium, England and Turkey in the knockout stages and eventually beat Germany 2-0 in the final to claim their fifth World Cup.

France and Italy put a disappointing Euro 2004 tournament behind them to progress to the 2006 World Cup final. Sadly, the match is best remembered for Zinedine Zidane's head-butt on Marco Materazzi rather than the goals they both scored in an exhilarating final. Italy won the decisive shootout to claim their fourth title. It was only the second World Cup final since 1938 not to feature either Brazil or Germany.

The 2010 World Cup final in Johannesburg was also marred by violence. Neither the Netherlands or Spain had won the tournament before, but the silky skills of the Spanish were expected to trump the work-rate and determination of the Dutch. As the sides had never met in the World Cup or European Championships,

however, it wasn't an easy match to predict. It immediately became clear that the Dutch were trying to out-muscle the Spanish and their ferocious – and at times illegal – tackling should have seen more than one player sent off. To his credit, referee Howard Webb tried to let the game flow but the Netherlands wouldn't play ball and forced him to dish out the yellow cards. It was something of a relief for the neutral when Andrés Iniesta scored the winner with four minutes of extra time remaining.

The 2014 World Cup will be held in Brazil, and several of the players featured in this compilation of the 100 greatest World Cup footballers will be hoping to cement their reputation by winning the sport's greatest prize.

# Ademir

Ademir enjoyed an 18-year domestic career with Sport Recife, Fluminese and Vasco da Gama, but it was his nine years with the latter club that defined him as a player of supreme skill and one of the greatest centre forwards in the game's history. He was quick over short distances and immensely powerful, and his sublime finishing elevated him above every other player in the world. In all he made 429 appearances for Vasco da Gama, scored 301 goals and secured five state championships.

He was called up to the national team in 1945 and made an impact in the Copa América (12 goals in 18 starts overall) with a tournament-winning hat-trick in 1949. In 1950 the World Cup came to Brazil and he partnered Zizinho and Jair in a deadly three-pronged attack. He scored an incredible 14 goals in nine starts during the build-up and in the tournament itself, including two in their opening match against Mexico, four against Sweden and another two against Spain. Sadly he couldn't prevent Uruguay winning the de facto final 2-1. The defeat weighed heavily on his mind and he didn't play at all the following year. He returned in 1952 but only managed another eight international appearances and three goals in the Copa América.

He retired from all football in 1957 to concentrate on commentating and coaching. How he must have enjoyed watching the team he had inspired lift the World Cup in Sweden in 1958.

**Name:** Ademir (Marques de Menezes)
**Born:** November 8th 1922, Recife, Brazil
**Died:** May 11th 1996, Rio de Janeiro
**Position:** Striker
**International Career:** 1945 – 1953
**Caps:** 39
**Goals:** 32
**Honours:** Copa América (1949), World Cup Runner-up and Golden Boot (1950)

# Alberto

Carlos Alberto signed for Fluminese when he was 19 and he racked up nearly 100 appearances and nine goals, but it was only when he moved to Santos three years later that he became a global superstar. In eight years for the club he made 445 appearances and scored a half-century of goals, and it was on the back of these performances that he cemented his place in the national team. (He had made the 44-man training squad for the 1966 World Cup in England but he wasn't included in the final 22, which was a surprising decision given his leadership and flair.)

When João Saldanha was tasked with restoring pride to the yellow jersey, he chose Carlos Alberto as the national captain. Four years later all the pieces were in place for the side to reap the benefits at the 1970 World Cup in Mexico. Perhaps the finest team assembled in the modern era romped through the initial group stage with wins over Romania, defending champions England and Czechoslovakia. With Carlos Alberto at the helm, the side then dispatched Peru (4-2), Uruguay (3-1) in the semi-final, and Italy (4-1) in a one-sided final. He scored the best goal of the tournament and one of the greatest goals of all-time after the ball had been passed around the entire team. When Pelé eventually laid the ball off on the edge of the Italian area, Carlos Alberto thundered in from right back and rifled the ball into the bottom corner of the net.

It was to be his only appearance at the World Cup, however, as a persistent knee injury ruled him out of the 1974 tournament in West Germany and seriously limited his speed down the flank when he was eventually passed fit. He was selected by coach Claudio Coutinho to captain the side in the first three qualifying matches for the 1978 World Cup but, as he hadn't played for seven years and was now 33, he'd lost his edge and retired to join former greats like Pelé and George Best at New York Cosmos.

He moved into coaching in 1983 with Flamengo and then flitted amongst a number of clubs before ending up as

# ALBERTO

**Right:** *Brazilian captain Carlos Alberto raises the Jules Rimet Trophy after his team's 4-1 victory over Italy in the 1970 World Cup final*

the national manager of Azerbaijan in 2005. He resigned after assaulting the technical referee and suggesting the match officials had been bribed when his side lost against Poland.

Apart from this brief controversy, Carlos Alberto's career only attracts the highest praise. He captained the greatest side in the world, was listed as one of Pelé's greatest living footballers in 2004 and was then included in the World Team of the 20th Century. If his knee hadn't kept him out of the national team

for seven years, he would surely rank alongside Pelé, Maradona, Messi and Cristiano Ronaldo as one of the greatest players of all time.

**Name:** Carlos Alberto (Torres)
**Born:** July 17th 1944, Rio de Janeiro, Brazil
**Position:** Right back
**International Career:** 1964 – 1977
**Caps:** 53
**Goals:** 8
**Honours:** World Cup Winner (1970)

# Baggio

Roberto Baggio played for his local youth side for nine years before he was spotted by scout Antonio Mora and signed by Vicenza. His early career was almost derailed by a serious knee injury but when he'd recovered he moved to Fiorentina and scored 39 league goals in 94 starts. This form brought him to the attention of Juventus and he signed for a world-record fee of £8 million in 1990.

Azeglio Vicini called him up to the national squad in 1988 but he had to wait a year for his first goal, which he scored against Uruguay in a friendly. Later that year he scored Italy's 500th goal, and he was on target again during Italia '90. In their group match against Czechoslovakia, Baggio beat several defenders and slotted the ball home for one of the tournament's greatest individual goals. Italy then overcame Uruguay and the Republic of Ireland to set up a semi-final with Maradona's Argentina, which the South Americans won on penalties. Baggio then scored once more against England in the third-place playoff.

Italy squeezed through their group at the 1994 World Cup and a brace from Baggio then saw off Nigeria. He also scored the winner against Spain in the quarter-final and another brace against Bulgaria in the semi to set up a final against Brazil. The game was hardly a classic and remained goal-less after extra time. Baggio, who was carrying a hamstring injury, then missed the decisive penalty in the shootout.

Baggio was left out of the national side for much of the next four years but Cesare Maldini recalled him for France '98. His penalty against Chile meant he became the first Italian to score at three World Cups, and he helped the side finish top of their group after scoring again against Austria. Alessandro Del Piero then returned from injury and Baggio had to make do with coming off the bench against France in the quarter-final. This time he scored his penalty in the resulting shootout but Albertini and Di Biagio missed theirs and Italy were eliminated.

Baggio was hardly used in the next

**Right:** *Brazilian goalkeeper Cláudio Taffarel dives the wrong way but Roberto Baggio's penalty goes over the crossbar and Italy lose the 1994 World Cup final*

six years, although he was given an international send-off against Spain in 2004. He was technically gifted and had great vision and awareness, which allowed him to play a roving role behind a lone striker. In a senior career spanning more than two decades, he scored 318 goals in 693 appearances.

**Name:** Roberto Baggio
**Born:** February 18th 1967, Caldogno, Italy
**Position:** Striker
**International Career:** 1988 – 2004
**Caps:** 56
**Goals:** 27
**Honours:** World Cup Runner-up and World Cup All-Star Team (1994)

# Banks

England's finest goalkeeper was born in Yorkshire. His father managed an illegal betting shop which allowed the family to live relatively comfortably, although this prosperity came at great personal cost: his disabled brother was mugged for the daily take and later died of his injuries. Working as a bagger for a coal merchant and a hod carrier allowed him to develop great upper-body strength, and he was soon playing for Rawmarsh and then Millspaugh.

Chesterfield spotted him in 1953 and offered him a trial in their youth team, which led to a £3/week contract. After his national service, he helped the side to the final of the 1956 FA Youth Cup, which ended in a narrow defeat to the Busby Babes. He graduated to the senior team in 1958-9 and was shocked when First Division club Leicester then paid £7,000 for him.

Despite several poor performances, he worked on his weaknesses in his spare time and developed into a vocal keeper of considerable ability. Leicester finished

sixth in the league in 1960-61 and only lost to the all-conquering Spurs in the FA Cup final. Two years later he made his international debut under Alf Ramsey in a 2-1 defeat to Scotland at Wembley.

Banks quickly established himself as the nation's best keeper and he only conceded one goal en route to the World Cup final in 1966. Although he was beaten twice in the final itself, England put four past West Germany and lifted the Jules Rimet Trophy. Banks was again inspirational four years later during England's defence of the crown. In the second group match

**Above:** *Gordon Banks makes the most famous save in football history from a Pelé header during England's epic match against Brazil at the 1970 World Cup*

against Brazil, he pulled off the greatest save in football history when he denied Pelé a certain goal by flicking his powerful header over the bar from an impossible angle. Unfortunately, Banks then suffered a bout of food poisoning and missed the quarter-final against West Germany. Despite taking a 2-0 lead, the Germans rallied and put three past Peter Bonetti.

In 1972, Banks was forced to retire after a car crash robbed him of the sight in one eye. In his 73 international appearances he kept 35 clean sheets and only lost nine games, an incredible record for one of the game's greatest goalkeepers.

**Name:** Gordon Banks, OBE
**Born:** December 30th 1937, Sheffield, England
**Position:** Goalkeeper
**International Career:** 1963 - 1972
**Caps:** 73
**Goals:** 0
**Honours:** World Cup Winner (1966)

# Baresi

Goalkeepers and defenders rarely attain the hero status afforded to strikers but Franco Baresi was an exceptional sweeper for AC Milan and marshalled one of the finest defences in the game. His pinpoint tackling and ability on the ball made him one of the best defenders in the world for more than a decade.

Baresi was born in May 1960 in Travagliato in northern Italy. His parents died when he was in his teens so he looked for an outlet in football. Internazionale rejected him so he tried to join rivals AC Milan, eventually succeeding after his third trial at the age of 14. He soon established himself in the first team as Milan won the Scudetto (Serie A championship), and so began a lifelong association with the club. Baresi became known as the Steel Man, leading what many believe to be the best back four in the history of the game (alongside Paolo Maldini, Allesandro Costacurta and Mauro Tassotti).

The club was found guilty of match-rigging in 1980, so they were fined and relegated to Serie B but Silvio Berlusconi stepped in, bringing in a relatively unknown manager, Arrigo Sacchi, while also spending money on transfers. With Baresi as captain, the team won the Italian league five times in the late 1980s and early 1990s; the European Champions Cup in 1989, 1990 and 1994; as well as the Intercontinental Cup in 1989 and again in 1990. When he hung up his boots in 1997 after 719 games, the club retired the number six jersey in his honour.

Baresi came late to international football and he only made the bench during Italy's World Cup-winning run in Spain (1982). He made his debut against Romania later that year but refused to play while Bearzot was in charge, which meant he missed the 1986 finals in Mexico. With Baresi at the centre of their defence, the Azzurri reached the semi-finals of the 1988 European Championships in West Germany before losing to the USSR. In the 1990 World Cup in his home county, Italy reached the semi-finals before losing

**Above:** *Franco Baresi of Italy is closed down by Stuart McCall of Scotland*

to Argentina. They then beat England to finish third after a play-off.

Despite a slow start at the 1994 World Cup in the USA, Baresi captained his side during a cautious final against Brazil that ended 0-0. Baresi missed his penalty in the shoot-out and Roberto Baggio blasted his over the bar to hand victory to the South Americans.

After retiring, Baresi stayed in the game that he graced. He now works as a talent scout and youth team coach at his beloved AC Milan.

**Name:** Franco Baresi
**Born:** May 8th 1960, Travagliato, Italy
**Position:** Sweeper
**International Career:** 1982 - 1994
**Caps:** 82
**Goals:** 2
**Honours:** World Cup Winner (1982), World Cup Runner-up (1994)

# Beckenbauer

A true football legend, Der Kaiser won the World Cup as captain of the national side and then as its manager. In his prime, he read the game better than anyone and invented the attacking sweeper role. His precise passing, technical superiority and superb leadership made him the focal point for Bayern Munich and West Germany for nearly 20 years. As manager of the national team, he masterminded their World Cup victory at Italia '90.

Franz Anton Beckenbauer was born in 1945 in the ruins of post-war Munich. He started playing football for youth side SC Munich 1906 aged only eight. After impressing at an under-14s tournament, he decided to join Munich's second club, Bayern, in 1959. Three years later he gave up his job and became a professional player. Bayern won promotion to the top flight in his first full season.

By 1968-9, Beckenbauer, now captain, led the team to its first championship in 37 years. With him at the heart of the team, goal-machine Gerd Müller up front

and the excellent Sepp Maier between the sticks, Bayern dominated European club football throughout the early 1970s. In 1977, Beckenbauer stunned the world by signing for New York Cosmos in the North American League (along with Pelé) but he returned to Germany after four seasons.

Beckenbauer's international career was equally spectacular. In 1965 he earned the first of more than 100 caps and he played every game at the 1966 World Cup in England, scoring four goals before having to man-mark Bobby Charlton in the final. West Germany avenged the defeat by the hosts four years later when they knocked England out in the quarter-finals of Mexico '70 after being 2-0 down. Beckenbauer broke his collarbone against Italy in the semi-final but played on, although his team eventually lost a thrilling encounter 4-3.

Beckenbauer then led Germany to victory in the 1972 European Championships in Belgium with a convincing 3-0 win over the USSR in

**Above:** *Franz Beckenbauer (right) tackles a Dutch player during the 1974 World Cup final in Munich*

Czechoslovakia in the final.

Beckenbauer retired shortly afterwards but he was soon convinced to take over as national team coach. He promptly guided an average side to the World Cup final in Mexico in 1986, although they lost 3-2 to Argentina. In the 1988 European Championships, old rivals the Netherlands knocked them out in the semi-finals but, two years later, Beckenbauer completed a remarkable double by managing the team that won the World Cup in Italy, the only man to win the trophy as a captain and a manager.

Still an influential figure in European football, Beckenbauer returned to manage Bayern Munich before becoming club president. He helped organise the bid for the 2006 World Cup in Germany.

the final. They backed this up with a superb display as hosts of the 1974 World Cup. Although they trailed to the mighty Dutch in the final, the Germans remained calm and fought back to win 2-1. They showed the same determination in the semi-final of the 1976 European Championships in Yugoslavia when they came from 2-0 down to beat the hosts 4-2 in extra time, although they then lost to

**Name:** Franz Anton Beckenbauer
**Born:** September 11th 1945, Munich, Germany
**Position:** Sweeper
**International Career:** 1965 - 1977
**Caps:** 103
**Goals:** 14
**Honours:** European Championship Winner (1972), World Cup Winner (1974), World Cup-Winning Coach (1990)

# Beckham

The David Beckham brand is known the world over and is not confined to football. His face is recognised by millions, his life dissected by the frantic media, but, despite all the attention, he remains the consummate football professional. His time in the sport has included the lows of red cards in high-profile matches and the highs of single-handedly dragging the national team to the 2002 World Cup in the Far East.

Beckham was born in Leytonstone in May 1975. Unusually for a boy growing up in East London, he became obsessed with Manchester United and aged 12 he enrolled at one of Bobby Charlton's youth football schools in the city alongside future internationals Ryan Giggs, Paul Scholes, Gary Neville, Nicky Butt, Keith Gillespie and Robbie Savage. In 1992 he made his first-team debut against Brighton & Hove Albion in the League Cup before being loaned to Preston North End. He then returned to United and made his league debut against Leeds in 1994-95.

With Beckham playing an increasingly important midfield role, United won the Premier League and FA Cup double in 1996. Later that year he made his international debut against Moldova in a World Cup qualifier. The following year United defended the league title and Beckham was awarded the PFA Young Player of the Year.

His stock increased further when it emerged that he was dating Victoria Adams of the Spice Girls, but he was left on the bench for England's opening matches at the 1998 World Cup. Beckham then became a national hero when he scored against Colombia and secured their progress to the knockout stages, but hero turned villain when he was sent off against Argentina for deliberately kicking Diego Simeone. England lost on penalties and Beckham became public enemy number one.

Sir Alex Ferguson managed to get the best out of him on the domestic front and he was instrumental in helping United secure the elusive treble in 1999: the English Premier League; the FA Cup; and, in an epic final, the European Champions Cup against Bayern Munich in Barcelona.

On the international front, however, the

France and the side then lost a shootout in the quarter-final to hosts Portugal.

England's confidence before the 2006 World Cup in Germany was also misplaced and the side was knocked out on penalties. Beckham stepped down as captain and new manager Steve McClaren then dropped him from the squad, as did domestic manager Fabio Capello at Real Madrid. So, in January 2007, Beckham signed a five-year contract with Los Angeles Galaxy. His international career looked to be over but he soon became England's most capped outfield player, although he then missed out on the national squad for the 2012 European Championships and the London Olympics.

Beckham has now established several football academies in East London and Los Angeles, and he helped promote London's successful 2012 Olympic bid, as well as becoming a Goodwill Ambassador for the United Nation's Children Fund (UNICEF).

public were yet to forgive him and the 2000 European Championships were a disaster. His redemption came first in Munich – where England thrashed Germany 5-1 – and then at Old Trafford when, as captain of his country, he secured England's place at the 2002 World Cup with the finest individual performance of his career, his last-minute free-kick sending a nation delirious, although England lost to eventual winners Brazil in the quarter-final of the tournament proper.

After a poor start to the 2003 season, United regained the league title but, after 394 appearances and 85 goals, Real Madrid signed Beckham for £25 million. The fans took to him but the team didn't capture a major trophy. Euro 2004 in Portugal was another disappointment for Beckham. His penalty was saved in England's 2-1 defeat by

| | |
|---|---|
| **Name:** | David Robert Joseph Beckham OBE |
| **Born:** | May 2nd 1975, London, England |
| **Position:** | Midfield |
| **International Career:** | 1996 - 2009 |
| **Caps:** | 115 |
| **Goals:** | 17 |
| **Honours:** | Le Tournoi (1997) |

# Bergomi

Giuseppe Bergomi joined Internazionale at the age of 16 and made his professional debut the following season. Within a year he'd been called up to the Italian national team, but he suffered a loss on debut to East Germany in a friendly before the 1982 World Cup in Spain. Italy drew all three of their group matches and were fortunate to progress, but then they exploded into life with dazzling wins over Argentina and Brazil.

Bergomi was rock solid at the back in the 2-0 semi-final win over Poland, and he was again on hand to limit the West Germans to a single goal in the final. Paolo Rossi, Marco Tardelli and Alessandro Altobelli scored for Italy and the Azzurri lifted the FIFA World Cup. He was selected for the 1986 World Cup in Mexico but Italy were knocked out by France in the round of 16. Italy made the semi-final of Euro '88, after which Bergomi was chosen to captain the side for the World Cup on home soil. The Azzurri won their three group matches and the first two knockout games without conceding a goal, but they came unstuck against Maradona's Argentina in the semi-final and went out on penalties. Italy then beat England in the playoff to claim third place overall.

Bergomi was sent off during a qualifying match for Euro '92 and didn't earn a recall for nearly six years, robbing him of countless caps but thankfully not affecting his contribution to the world game. Italy topped their group at France '98 but went out to the hosts on penalties in the quarter-final. It was Bergomi's last appearance for the national team. He played on at domestic level for another year before finally hanging up his boots after 756 appearances and 28 goals.

**Name:** Giuseppe 'Beppe' Bergomi
**Born:** December 22nd 1963, Milan, Italy
**Position:** Defender
**International Career:** 1982 - 1998
**Caps:** 81
**Goals:** 6
**Honours:** World Cup Winner (1982)

# Bergkamp

Dennis Bergkamp was born in a working-class suburb of Amsterdam and he soon joined the Ajax youth team. He made his professional debut under Johan Cruyff in 1986 but had to wait until the following year to score his first senior goal. He helped the side win the 1992 UEFA Cup and the domestic KNVB Trophy, which earned him the Dutch footballer of the year accolade.

He signed for Internazionale in 1993 but his time in Italy was unsuccessful and he then joined Arsenal. It was no coincidence that Bergkamp's skill, positional awareness and precise passing and shooting raised the bar for the other players, and Arsenal – now under new coach Arsène Wenger – were suddenly transformed into one of the best teams in the Premier League.

Bergkamp was picked for the national team after the World Cup in 1990. He scored three goals at Euro '92 but couldn't help a strong Dutch side defend the trophy and they went out to Denmark on penalties. He was on superb form at the 1994 World Cup in the USA and helped the side to the latter stages with goals against Morocco and the Republic of Ireland. He scored again against Brazil in the quarter-final but two late Bebeto strikes won the best game of the tournament for the South Americans.

The Dutch were off the pace during Euro '96 but Bergkamp rediscovered his scintillating club form at the World Cup in France two years later. They topped their group with two draws and a 5-0 demolition of South Korea, and Bergkamp scored against Yugoslavia in the round of 16 to set up a clash with Argentina. He rates his winning goal in the last minute of that match as the best of his career. He controlled a 60-yard pass from Frank de Boer with one touch, knocked it through the defender's legs with his second and then fired into the top corner with the outside of his right foot. He scored his penalty against Brazil in the semi-final

shootout but Cocu and Ronald de Boer missed theirs and the Netherlands were eliminated.

He announced his international retirement after the Dutch were knocked out of Euro 2000 by Italy in the semi-final, but he played on for another six productive years with Arsenal. He lit up the league with his total-football style of play, devastating finishing and incredible skill, and he paved the way for most of the foreign stars in the English game. In 2011 he joined Ajax as an assistant coach.

**Name:** Dennis Nicolaas Bergkamp
**Born:** May 10th 1969, Amsterdam, Netherlands
**Position:** Second striker
**International Career:** 1990 – 2000
**Caps:** 79
**Goals:** 37
**Honours:** World Cup All-Star Team (1998)

# Blanc

In a playing career spanning more than 20 years, Blanc racked up more than 600 league appearances and 150 goals, an impressive haul for a defender. He made 97 starts for his country and was integral to the victorious World Cup and European Championship sides in 1998 and 2000.

Laurent Robert Blanc was born in November 1965 in Alès, France. He joined the Montpellier youth team in 1981 and graduated to the senior side as an offensive midfielder two years later. His eight years at the club yielded 300 appearances and more than 100 goals, and, having been persuaded to move into the defence, he was lured to Napoli for a season.

He returned to French outfit Nîmes the following year but moved again, to Saint-Étienne, in 1993. He then helped Auxerre to a league and cup double in 1995-6. After an unhappy year with Barcelona he moved to Marseille and then Internazionale, where he was voted club player of the year. He then moved again, this time to Manchester United. He was criticised for his first few performances but he was the rock in defence for the Premier League–winning campaign in 2002-3. He retired at the end of the season.

If his domestic career was punctuated with highs and lows and regular moves, his international career was littered with success and relatively stable. He made his French debut in 1989 but the side failed to qualify for the 1990 World Cup. With Blanc at the heart of the side, however, the French then went on a 19-game unbeaten streak that saw them emerge as joint favourites for the 1992 European Championships. Eventual winners Denmark knocked them out in the pool stages, however.

After another poor run of performances saw them fail to reach USA '94, Blanc announced his international retirement, but new coach Aimé Jacquet convinced him otherwise and he became an integral part of the Euro '96 and 1998 World Cup squads. During the latter tournament,

Blanc scored the first golden goal in the competition's history when the French knocked out Paraguay. Sadly for him, he missed the final after being sent of against Croatia in the semi-final. Despite being criticised for his age and lack of pace, he was solid throughout the victorious Euro 2000 campaign and he retired on a high at the end of the tournament.

Blanc moved into management in 2007 and he brought success to Bordeaux the following year when they won the league and cup double. In 2010 Blanc was named as the new manager of France. He guided them to the top of their group and qualification for Euro 2012. France were beaten 2-0 by Spain in the quarter-final and Blanc stepped down after the tournament.

| | |
|---|---|
| **Name:** | Laurent Robert Blanc |
| **Born:** | November 19th 1965, Alès, France |
| **Position:** | Defender |
| **International Career:** | 1989 - 2000 |
| **Caps:** | 97 |
| **Goals:** | 16 |
| **Honours:** | World Cup Winner (1998), European Championship Winner (2000) |

# Boniek

**Below:** *Zbigniew Boniek*

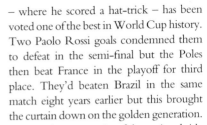

Zbigniew Boniek played with his local youth club until being signed by Widzew Łódz in 1975. Over the next seven years he scored 50 league goals in 172 starts before joining Italian giants Juventus. While in Turin, he helped the side to the 1984 Cup Winners' Cup and European Super Cup, and the European Cup the following season.

He was first selected for the national team in 1976 and, two years later, he scored twice against Mexico to ensure that Poland topped their group at the World Cup in Argentina. This was a golden era for Polish football, and, with Grzegorz Lato alongside Boniek, the side boasted a formidable frontline. Poland beat Peru in the second group phase but losses to hosts Argentina and then Brazil saw them eliminated.

Poland failed to qualify for the 1980 European Championships but the side topped their group again at the 1982 World Cup after another Boniek goal helped them demolish Peru 5-1. Boniek was a superb dribbler with great acceleration and vision, and his individual performance in the second-round match against Belgium – where he scored a hat-trick – has been voted one of the best in World Cup history. Two Paolo Rossi goals condemned them to defeat in the semi-final but the Poles then beat France in the playoff for third place. They'd beaten Brazil in the same match eight years earlier but this brought the curtain down on the golden generation.

Boniek was captain of the national side for Mexico '86 but Poland only squeezed through their group with a late winner over Portugal. They were then thumped 4-0 by Brazil in the round of 16 and Boniek retired from international football after Poland failed to qualify for Euro '88. He played on domestically with Roma until the end of the season before moving into management in 1990. He took charge of the national team in 2002 but resigned after only five games. At the end of Euro 2012, which had been co-hosted by Poland and the Ukraine, he became Chairman of the Polish Football Association.

| | |
|---|---|
| **Name:** | Zbigniew Kazimierz Boniek |
| **Born:** | March 3rd 1956, Bydgoszcz, Poland |
| **Position:** | Attacking midfield |
| **International Career:** | 1976 - 1988 |
| **Caps:** | 80 |
| **Goals:** | 24 |
| **Honours:** | World Cup Third Place (1982) |

# Breitner

Paul Breitner began his career as a mobile and tactically aware left back who was as likely to pop up and score goals as he was to make perfectly timed tackles in his own penalty area. He joined Bayern Munich at the age of 19 and only two years later he was part of the West German team that won the European Championship. He enjoyed more early success when he helped the national side lift the World Cup on home soil with victory over the much-fancied Dutch. It was his penalty that brought the hosts level and gave the side the confidence to overcome the total football of the opposition.

He moved from Munich to Real Madrid after the tournament and then surprised everyone further by announcing he was unavailable for the national squad. This self-imposed exile lasted until Jupp Derwall convinced him to return during the build-up to the 1982 World Cup in Spain. A typically robust and efficient West German side made it to the final and Breitner became only the third player to score in two World Cup finals (after Pelé and Vavá, although Zinedine Zidane has since become the fourth). It was in a losing cause, however, as Italy were crowned champions.

Often a controversial figure, his skill and technique were never in doubt, and his tally of more than 100 goals in a little over 400 games saw him justifiably selected as European Footballer of the Year in 1981. He was also chosen in the FIFA World Cup All-Time Team.

---

**Name:** Paul Breitner
**Born:** September 5th 1951, Kolbemoor, West Germany
**Position:** Left back, midfielder
**International Career:** 1971 - 1982
**Caps:** 48
**Goals:** 10
**Honours:** European Championship Winner (1972), World Cup Winner (1974), World Cup Runner-up (1982)

---

# Cafu

Cafu was raised in the Jardim Irene favela in São Paulo, but he soon developed into a footballer of considerable ability. By the age of seven he had enrolled with a football academy but he was then rejected by the Corinthian, Santos and Portuguesa youth teams. Instead, he found himself on the bench for the São Paulo juniors. Coach Telê Santana then suggested he try playing wing-back instead of midfield and Cafu immediately repaid Santana's faith by guiding the senior team to two Copa Libertadores (1992, 1993) and being named South American Footballer of the Year (1994).

He'd been called up by the national team in 1990 but he couldn't cement his place in the side and was only a substitute at the 1994 World Cup in the USA. However, an injury to Jorginho early in the final against Italy meant he got to play the next 100 minutes. The game went to penalties and Brazil lifted the trophy after Roberto Baggio's miss. Cafu was a revelation and was rarely out of the national team for the next 12 years.

He guided the team to his second World Cup final four years later in Paris against hosts France, but Brazil were off their game because star striker Ronaldo had suffered a seizure in the build-up. The qualifying campaign for the next tournament saw Cafu sent off against Paraguay and then stripped of the captaincy by Wanderley Luxemburgo. When the coach was dismissed, new manager Luiz Felipe Scolari chose Émerson as his captain but the skipper dislocated his shoulder in training and Cafu regained the armband.

He was again inspirational and led the team to his third World Cup final, a unique achievement by a player. He lifted the trophy after Brazil's 2-0 victory over Germany, but thereafter the team's fortunes declined and he was partially blamed for its poor performance at the 2006 World Cup in Germany. Coach Carlos Alberto Parreira was heavily criticised for relying on veterans like Cafu and Roberto Carlos and Brazil

**Left:** *Brazil celebrate as Cafu lifts the trophy after their 2-0 victory over Germany in the 2002 World Cup final*

were beaten 1-0 by France in the quarter-final.

Cafu initially wanted to continue until the 2010 World Cup in South Africa but by then his club career, which had been suitably glittering with Roma (Scudetto in 2001) and Milan (Scudetto in 2004 and Champions League in 2007), was in decline and he retired from football in 2008. He remains the only man to have played in three World Cup finals and his blistering pace, overlapping runs, leadership and honours for club and country ensure that he will forever be regarded as one of the great right backs and captains.

**Name:** Cafu (Marcos Evangelista de Moraes)
**Born:** June 7th 1970, São Paulo, Brazil
**Position:** Right back
**International Career:** 1990 – 2006
**Caps:** 142
**Goals:** 5
**Honours:** World Cup Winner (1994, 2002)

# Cannavaro

Fabio Cannavaro played for youth team Bagnoli before being spotted by scouts from Napoli. He was initially only a ball boy to the likes of Diego Maradona and Ciro Ferrara, and he once tackled Maradona so ferociously that the Napoli team rounded on him. Maradona, however, defended Cannavaro and the youngster soon graduated to the first team. He was so impressive that the side was forced to sell him on in a big-money move to Parma to raise funds after the departure of Maradona. There he joined Gianluigi Buffon, Roberto Mussi, Lilian Thuram and Néstor Sensini, which became one of the meanest defences in Europe.

He made his debut for the national team in 1997 but only announced himself on the world stage when he nullified Alan Shearer in a World Cup qualifier at Wembley. The tournament itself was a disappointment in that Italy were knocked out by hosts France in a quarter-final penalty shootout, but Cannavaro was now mentioned in the same breath as his legendary team-mates, Bergomi, Maldini and Costacurta. The Italians suffered more heartbreak when they lost to a David Trezeguet Golden Goal in the final of Euro 2000. They went out of the 2002 World Cup in similar fashion to co-hosts South Korea, but Cannavaro's performances were never less than sensational and he was handed the captaincy after the tournament.

Euro 2004 brought more disappointment for the Azzurri. Cannavaro collected two yellow cards, sat out the final group match against Bulgaria and watched his side eliminated on goal difference. The 2006 World Cup brought a change in fortune. Cannavaro led the side by example with hard tackling, accurate passing and tactical nous. On the night of his 100th cap, he earned the nickname 'The Berlin Wall' as he denied the French time and space in his defensive third. With the game poised at 1-1 deep into extra time, Zinedine Zidane head-butted Marco

Materazzi and was sent off. The French lost their confidence and Trezeguet missed his spot-kick in the shootout. Cannavaro, therefore, became the first Italian since Dino Zoff in 1982 to lift the FIFA World Cup.

Cannavaro was injured for Euro 2008 but he returned to captain the national team at the 2010 World Cup in South Africa. The tournament was a disaster, however, with Italy being dumped out in the group stage. He announced his international retirement immediately having racked up a record 136 caps.

**Name:** Fabio Cannavaro
**Born:** September 13th 1973, Naples, Italy
**Position:** Central defender
**International Career:** 1997 - 2010
**Caps:** 136
**Goals:** 2
**Honours:** European Championship Runner-up (2000), World Cup Winner (2006)

**Above:** *Fabio Cannavaro (centre) celebrating with the trophy after the 2006 World Cup final*

# Carlos

Roberto Carlos was born in Garça near São Paulo in a poor neighbourhood and he spent his time doing odd jobs on a farm and playing football with friends. His domestic career began with União São João, for whom he made 33 appearances from 1991 to 1993 and scored 10 goals. He then signed for Palmeiras and Internazionale before agreeing a big-money move to Spanish giants Real Madrid in 1996. He made the left back position his own for the next 11 years, racking up 584 starts and scoring 71 goals for a side that won four La Liga titles and appeared in three Champions League finals.

Having been voted the best left back in the world alongside Paolo Maldini, Roberto Carlos was called up for the Brazil squad in 1992, although he wasn't selected for the World Cup in the USA two years later. He helped the side to the Copa América in 1997 and then scored a remarkable free-kick against France in Le Tournoi. He struck the ball with the outside of his left foot from about 35 yards and, although it initially appeared that it would fly well wide of Fabien Barthez's goal, it suddenly curled back into the bottom corner.

He played in all seven matches at France '98 but couldn't help a lacklustre Brazil still reeling from Ronaldo's shock collapse overcome the hosts in the final at the new Stade de France. He exorcised the demons four years later in the Far East and was voted into the World Cup's all-star team after Brazil had beaten Germany in the final, 2-0. He played in his third and last World Cup in Germany in 2006 but he was blamed by many fans for failing to mark Thierry Henry effectively in their 1-0 quarter-final loss to the French. Carlos reacted angrily to the criticism and announced his international retirement.

Having returned to Brazil in 2010 to play out his club days with Corinthians, Roberto Carlos hoped to feature in Dunga's squad for the upcoming World Cup in South Africa but he, along with Ronaldo and Ronaldinho, were not

included in the 23-man party. In 2011 he turned his attention to managing Anzhi Makhachkala, a side in the Russian top flight.

Roberto Carlos was a scintillating player with great skill, balance, power and pace. His ferocious shooting and longevity – during his career he amassed 820 appearances and 101 goals – mean he stands alongside Italy's Paolo Maldini as the greatest left back in the game's history.

**Name:** Roberto Carlos (da Silva Rocha)
**Born:** April 10th 1973, São Paulo, Brazil
**Position:** Left back
**International Career:** 1992 - 2006
**Caps:** 125
**Goals:** 11
**Honours:** World Cup Winner (2002)

# Charles

John Charles was a gifted and versatile player who was solid at the back and lethal up front. He joined Swansea's youth team in 1946 and was scouted by Leeds two years later. In eight years with the Yorkshire side he scored 150 league goals in 297 starts, and a big-money move to Juventus followed. Charles scored the winner in each of his first three matches and became an instant hero in Turin. His five years in Italy yielded another 105 goals and helped Juventus to three league championships and two Italian cups. In 1997 he was voted the best overseas player in the club's history.

His versatility earned him a call-up to the Welsh national team in 1950, but it wasn't until 1958 that the wider world learned about the gentle giant. Charles scored to secure a draw against a Hungary team that had reached the final of the previous World Cup, and the side then drew with Mexico. A third draw against hosts and eventual finalists Sweden meant Wales had to play Hungary again in a playoff. Wales went behind but won 2-1 to set up a quarter-final against Brazil.

Sadly for Charles he was injured in the playoff and missed the match with Brazil. Had he played, football history might have been quite different: Pelé scored the only goal and Wales were eliminated.

Opposing players and fans were unanimous in their praise for Charles, a man who was never booked in his career, was voted the best foreign player in Serie A history (ahead of Maradona, Platini, Van Basten and Zidane) 34 years after his last game, and who was selected by Jimmy Greaves and Bobby Robson in an all-time World XI. In 2001 he became the first non-Italian to be inducted into the Azzurri Hall of Fame. Allowing for the fact that he played much of his career as a central defender, his 348 goals in 721 appearances elevate him to the game's elite alongside George Best and Johan Cruyff.

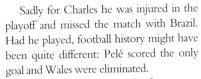

**Name:** (William) John Charles
**Born:** December 27th 1931, Swansea, Wales
**Died:** February 21st 2004, Wakefield, England
**Position:** Centre back / centre forward
**International Career:** 1950 – 1965
**Caps:** 38
**Goals:** 15
**Honours:** Serie A Winner (1958, 1960, 1961)

# Charlton

Sir Bobby Charlton is an English sporting hero. A gifted attacking midfielder with a devastating shot, he survived the Munich air disaster and helped Manchester United to league and European Cup glory, as well as being England's goal-scoring playmaker in 1966.

Robert Charlton was born into a football-mad family in Northumberland in October 1937 (his uncle was Newcastle United legend Jackie Milburn) and it was his mother, Cissie, who coached Bobby and brother Jack in their youth. Bobby was seen playing for East Northumberland schoolboys by a Manchester United talent scout and representatives from 18 clubs battled to secure his signature. At just 15, he signed for Manchester United, becoming one of the Busby Babes.

Charlton worked his way through the youth and reserve teams and eventually made his first-team debut in 1956. He scored twice and was soon holding down a regular place in the side that won the 1957 title. At Busby's insistence Manchester United entered the European Cup and were only narrowly defeated by the great Real Madrid side in the semi-final. The following season, United were returning home after their quarter-final victory against Red Star Belgrade when their plane crashed on take-off after a refuelling stop in Munich. Seven of Charlton's team-mates were killed instantly and Duncan Edwards died two weeks later. Despite the tragedy, United still competed well in the league and made it to the FA Cup final. At just 20, Charlton was now the key to Busby's Manchester United rebuilding program.

He made his international debut against Scotland later that year, and he was then named in the squad for the 1958 World Cup Finals in Sweden. He didn't play however, and England were eliminated in the group stages. The 1962 World Cup in Chile was also disappointing. Despite playing superbly, Charlton couldn't lift his team to beat Brazil.

On the domestic front, the addition of Nobby Stiles, Dennis Law and George

**Above:** *Bobby Charlton with his hundred England caps*

Portugal's Benfica 4-1 after extra time. Shortly afterwards, he also scored his 45th international goal, breaking Jimmy Greaves's record. Later that year, England were knocked out of the European Championships in the semi-finals, and both Bobby and Jack retired from international football after England's disappointing 1970 World Cup campaign in Mexico.

Charlton then founded several soccer coaching schools in the UK (where David Beckham was spotted), USA, Canada, Australia and China, before he became a director at Manchester United in 1984, a position he still holds. A true ambassador for English sport, Charlton was the driving force behind Manchester's Olympic bids in 1996 and 2000, as well as London's successful bid. As Sir Matt Busby once said, "He was as near perfection as a man and player as it is possible to be."

Best proved inspired and United won the league in 1965 and 1967, but the year in between was Charlton's annus mirabilis. He won the Football Writers' Player of the Year and European Footballer of the Year accolades, and he then guided the national side to World Cup glory. Franz Beckenbauer later reflected on the final against West Germany: "England beat us in 1966 because Bobby Charlton was just a bit better than me." The lynchpin of England's triumph, he was voted the best player in the tournament.

More silverware followed with the European Cup in 1968 as United became the first English team to lift the trophy. Charlton scored twice as United beat

**Name:** Sir Robert 'Bobby' Charlton CBE
**Born:** October 11th 1937, Ashington, England
**Position:** Attacking midfield
**International Career:** 1958 – 1970
**Caps:** 106
**Goals:** 49
**Honours:** World Cup Winner (1966)

# Cole

**Above:** *Ashley Cole*

Ashley Cole signed for Arsenal, the club he'd supported as a boy, in 1999 at the age of 18. He joined Crystal Palace for a short loan spell but then spent the next six years in North London with the Gunners. He developed into a solid left back with good awareness, a turn of pace that allowed him to break forward to support the strikers, and great tactical nous that allowed him to use his skill rather than strength to dispossess bigger opponents.

After only a handful of games for the England Under-21 side he was selected by Sven-Goran Eriksson for a match against Albania in 2001. He was always dependable in the group matches at the 2002 World Cup, although he couldn't stop Ronaldinho sliding the ball through to Rivaldo for the equaliser in the quarter-final. Ronaldinho then caught David Seaman out with a speculative free-kick and England were eliminated.

Cole was named in the all-star team of the tournament at Euro 2004 and he was again on top form at the 2006 World Cup, making a crucial block against Ecuador that helped England through to the knockout phase.

He was still in the side for the 2010 World Cup in South Africa, and he was one of the only players to emerge from the tournament in credit as England were humiliated by the Germans in the second phase. Indeed he is one of only three or four England players – along with Steven Gerrard, Frank Lampard and Wayne Rooney – of the current generation with genuine elite-level ability.

In 2006 he signed for Chelsea after a tapping-up scandal and even more scandalous wage demands, but he has repaid the faith for club and country many times. He holds the record for the most England appearances without scoring a goal, this despite him finding the net 20 times at domestic level.

---

**Name:** Ashley Cole
**Born:** December 20th 1980, London, England
**Position:** Left back
**International Career:** 2001 – present
**Caps:** 106
**Goals:** 0
**Honours:** FA Summer Tournament Winner (2004)

---

# Cruyff

The most gifted footballer of his generation, Johan Cruyff led the total football revolution with Ajax Amsterdam and the Netherlands in the 1970s. Blessed with exceptional skill, pinpoint passing and a terrific turn of speed, he became synonymous with the way the beautiful game should be played. He went on to lead Barcelona to domestic and European Cup triumphs as a visionary manager in the early 1990s.

Hendrik Johannes Cruyff was born in April 1947 in a suburb of Amsterdam. He enjoyed football from a young age and by his 10th birthday he'd been picked from over 200 children to join the Ajax youth team. Seven years later he was playing in Rinus Michels's revolutionary first team at Ajax Amsterdam that allowed the players to rotate positions in an adventurous and fluid style.

This suited Cruyff and he turned up all over the pitch and ran teams ragged. He made his debut against FC Groningen in 1964 and scored Ajax's only goal. After another 274 appearances, he'd scored a barely believable 204 goals. During this period, Ajax dominated both the Dutch league and Europe, where they won three consecutive European Cups.

In 1973 Cruyff followed Rinus Michels to Barcelona for a world-record fee of nearly a million pounds. His time in Spain allowed Barça to break Real Madrid's domination of La Liga and he lifted the league title in his first season. By performing consistently at the highest level domestically he was a shoe-in for the national team and the Dutch were favourites for the 1974 World Cup in Germany. The other teams couldn't cope with their pace and passing and they demolished everyone before meeting the hosts in the final.

The match was billed as a contest between the German efficiency of Franz Beckenbauer and the precocious ability of Cruyff's Dutch. The Dutch scored before the Germans had touched the ball but they couldn't finish the Germans off and Beckenbauer began to dominate the midfield. The home side went on to win 2-1.

Cruyff scored five goals and was

**Left:** *Johan Cruyff
bursts into the
West German
penalty area in the
opening seconds
of the 1974 World
Cup final*

inspirational in helping his side to the 1976 European Championships in Yugoslavia but the tournament was disappointing and he retired before the 1978 World Cup Finals in Argentina.

He then made a much-publicised move to the North American Soccer League but, despite the big names who went with him (Pelé, Beckenbauer, George Best, Bobby Moore), the project failed. He returned to Europe to see out his club career and hung up his boots in 1984. He soon took over as manager of Ajax and led them to the KNVB Beker trophy. He also won the European Cup Winners' Cup in 1987. Having moved to Barcelona, he guided the Catalan giants to four consecutive league titles, the Spanish Cup, the Cup Winners' Cup, and the Champions Cup.

He set up the Johan Cruyff Foundation in 1997, which helps improve the lives of underprivileged children.

| | |
|---|---|
| **Name:** | Hendrik Johannes 'Johan' Cruyff |
| **Born:** | April 25th 1947, Amsterdam, Netherlands |
| **Position:** | Attacking midfield |
| **International Career:** | 1966 – 1977 |
| **Caps:** | 48 |
| **Goals:** | 33 |
| **Honours:** | World Cup Runner-up (1974) |

# Cubillas

**Below:** *Teófilo Cubillas*

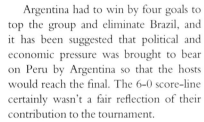

Teófilo Cubillas joined youth side Alianza Lima before graduating to the senior team in 1966. He was the top scorer in the league in his debut season and eventually netted 116 goals in 175 appearances for the club. He was called up to the national team in 1968 and scored in all four of Peru's matches at the 1970 World Cup in Mexico. After qualifying from a tough group, Peru faced Brazil in the quarter-final. Cubillas scored a late goal to give Peru hope but Jairzinho sealed the win for the eventual champions five minutes later.

The national team failed to qualify for the 1974 World Cup but Peru lifted the Copa América in 1975 after Cubillas scored again against Brazil. Three years later he scored another five goals as Peru beat Scotland and Iran to reach the second group stage of the 1978 World Cup. There was no disgrace in losing to Brazil or a Polish side packed with gifted players during their golden generation, but their capitulation against hosts Argentina in their last match has never been satisfactorily explained.

Argentina had to win by four goals to top the group and eliminate Brazil, and it has been suggested that political and economic pressure was brought to bear on Peru by Argentina so that the hosts would reach the final. The 6-0 score-line certainly wasn't a fair reflection of their contribution to the tournament.

Cubillas played the three group matches at the next World Cup in Spain but he failed to find the target and Peru were eliminated after losing 5-1 to Poland. He retired from international football but played on domestically in North America until 1989. Records of his achievements are incomplete but he probably scored more than 400 goals in 650 appearances.

**Name:** Teófilo Juan Cubillas (Arizaga)
**Born:** March 8th 1949, Lima, Peru
**Position:** Forward
**International Career:** 1968 - 1982
**Caps:** 81
**Goals:** 26
**Honours:** World Cup All-Star Team (1970, 1978)

# Deschamps

A defensive midfielder with a superb touch, good pace and great tactical awareness, Deschamps will be forever remembered as the man who captained France to World Cup glory in 1998 and repeated the feat on the European stage two years later. It could all have been different, however, if he'd stuck to rugby in his youth.

Didier Claude Deschamps was born in Bayonne in October 1968. He was drawn to the oval ball game but was lured from Olympique Biarritz by amateur football side Aviron Bayonnais as a schoolboy. He was then spotted by scouts from Nantes in 1983 and he made his league debut two years later. He spent a couple of years with the club before transferring to Marseille and helping them to two league titles and the Champions League in 1993.

It was only a matter of time before the inspirational young captain was snapped up by one of the top clubs in Italy, Spain or England, and Deschamps chose Juventus. He helped the side win seven trophies in five years before moving to Chelsea, where he won the FA Cup in 2000. He then enjoyed a short spell in Spain with Valencia before hanging up his playing boots at the comparatively young age of thirty-two.

Although he could list a great many domestic triumphs on his CV, it was on the international stage that Deschamps became immortalised. He was given his first cap by Michel Platini in 1989 but France were a poor side in transition and they failed to qualify for the World Cup in 1990 and 1994. He was almost dropped from the side when Aimé Jacquet began rebuilding for the 1998 World Cup in France but he was one of the veterans who survived the chop while Cantona and Ginola did not.

As captain of a golden generation that included the likes of Zinedine Zidane, Patrick Vieira and Thierry Henry, Deschamps led the side to the semi-final of Euro '96. On home soil two years later, the French brushed aside all-comers and then defeated Brazil 3-0 in the World

**Above:** *Didier Deschamps of France holds the trophy after the 2000 European Championships*

Having retired, Deschamps immediately took to management, guiding AS Monaco to their first appearance in the Champions League final. He then moved back to Juventus, a club in disarray after a match-fixing scandal had seen the side relegated to Serie B. Deschamps led them back into the top flight but resigned immediately afterwards citing difficulties with the club's board. Deschamps then oversaw Marseille's first league title in 18 years. He left the club in 2012 to take over as coach of the national side and he oversaw their qualification to the 2014 World Cup in Brazil.

Cup final at the Stade de France. Euro 2000 was equally successful, France beating Italy with an extra-time Golden-Goal winner from David Trezeguet in the final in Rotterdam.

**Name:** Didier Claude Deschamps
**Born:** October 15th 1968, Bayonne, France
**Position:** Defensive midfield
**International Career:** 1989 - 2000
**Caps:** 103
**Goals:** 4
**Honours:** World Cup Winner (1998), European Championship Winner (2000)

# Didi

Didi almost lost his right leg when he picked up a serious infection in his teens, but he recovered and turned professional in 1946. He didn't make much of an impact until he signed for Fluminese in 1949. He missed out on the 1950 World Cup but was selected four years later and he scored goals against Mexico and Yugoslavia before Brazil were beaten by Hungary in the infamous 'Battle of Bern'.

In 1958 he masterminded the first of two Brazilian World Cup triumphs. He was instrumental in the side reaching the final in Sweden and was then voted the best player in the tournament. He was also inspirational in the 1962 event in Chile, scoring several remarkable goals and helping Brazil to consecutive World Cup wins. He retired from international football immediately afterwards but he continued his domestic career with Botafogo, Sporting Cristal, São Paulo and CD Veracruz.

He'd first tried management with Cristal in 1962 and he then coached another eight teams – including Peru at the 1970 World Cup – before finally retiring in 1986. Didi was an exquisite footballer with great stamina and flawless technique, and he had the ability to pick out impossible passes. He also pioneered several different free-kicks with varying amounts of bend and dip.

**Name:** Didi (Waldyr Pereira)
**Born:** October 8th 1928, Campos dos Goytacazes, Brazil
**Died:** May 12th 2001, Rio de Janeiro
**Position:** Central midfield
**International Career:** 1952 - 1962
**Caps:** 68
**Goals:** 20
**Honours:** World Cup Winner (1958, 1962)

# Džajić

**Below:** *Dragan Džajić*

Dragan Džajić joined Red Star Belgrade as a youth in 1961. Two years later he made the first of 590 senior league appearances. Over the next 12 years he scored an incredible 365 goals for the team and helped them to five league titles and four Yugoslav cups. He developed into a player who could use both feet equally well, whether passing or dribbling, although he was young and inexperienced when he made his international debut in a 2-1 defeat to Romania in 1964.

Four years later Džajić scored a beautiful chip against England in the semi-final of the European Championships. He scored again in the final against Italy but the game finished 1-1 and Italy won the replay 2-0. The English press were so impressed that they dubbed him the 'Magic Dragan', while Pelé called him a Balkan miracle: "I'm sorry he's not Brazilian because I've never seen such a natural footballer." High praise indeed.

Džajić guided Yugoslavia to the top of their group (above Brazil) at the 1974 World Cup, and he scored one of Yugoslavia's record nine goals against Zaire. But a strong team then inexplicably lost all three of its matches in the second phase. He was inspirational at the 1976 European Championships and singlehandedly dismantled West Germany in the semi-final, only for the Germans to rally and force extra time. Yugoslavia eventually lost the match 4-2 and Džajić retired from international football two years later.

Džajić stayed with Red Star as technical director but he was put on trial for fraud over his involvement in the sale of players like Nemanja Vidic during his time as club president. All of the charges were eventually dropped and Džajić was elected president of the club for the third time in 2012.

**Name:** Dragan Džajić
**Born:** May 30th 1946, Ub, Yugoslavia
**Position:** Left wing
**International Career:** 1964 – 1978
**Caps:** 85
**Goals:** 23
**Honours:** European Championship Runner-up (1968)

# Eusébio

Nicknamed the Black Pearl, Mozambique-born Eusébio became a legendary player for Benfica and Portugal in the 1960s. The striker was quick and possessed a fierce right-foot shot. He made a name for himself on the world stage during the 1966 World Cup in England when he single-handedly guided his side to the semi-final after superb performances against Brazil and North Korea.

Eusébio de Silva Ferreira was born in January 1942 in a poor district of the capital of Mozambique, then a Portuguese colony. He was an excellent young sportsman and began his football career with Sporting Clube de Lorenço Marques. Brazilian coach Bauer soon spotted him but Brazil's club sides weren't interested and it wasn't until Benfica's coach Bela Guttman saw him play that he was signed.

Eusébio blossomed into a fine footballer at Benfica and he scored twice in the 1962 European Champions Cup final as his team beat the all-conquering Real Madrid side of Ferenc Puskás and Alfredo di Stéfano. His prolific goal-scoring record over the following four seasons earned him his first European Footballer of the Year title in 1965. Benfica went on to dominate their domestic league, winning it 11 times, as well as the Portuguese Cup five times.

Eusébio made his international debut for Portugal in a World Cup qualifying match against Luxemburg, which they lost despite being heavy favourites. By the 1966 World Cup, however, Eusébio's Portugal were a more potent force and they beat Hungary 3-1, and then demolished Bulgaria. Then they eliminated Brazil, champions in 1958 and 1962, with Eusébio scoring twice. North Korea surprised them in the quarter-final by taking a 3-0 lead but Eusébio rescued Portugal with four of his country's five goals. He scored again against England in the semi-final but they eventually lost 2-1. Sadly for fans of this little genius, this would be the only international tournament in which he would play.

He retired from top-flight domestic football in 1974 after a bad knee injury, but

**Right:** *The incomparable Eusébio*

that didn't stop him heading for the North American League before finally calling it a day in 1978. With 768 goals in 779 senior appearances, Eusébio is recognised as one of the game's all-time greats alongside Pelé, Maradona and Cruyff. The Portuguese government declared three days of national mourning when he passed away early in 2014.

**Name:** Eusébio da Silva Ferreira
**Born:** January 25th 1942, Portuguese East Africa
**Died:** January 5th 2014, Lisbon, Portugal
**Position:** Forward
**International Career:** 1961 – 1973
**Caps:** 64
**Goals:** 41
**Honours:** World Cup Third Place (1966)

# Facchetti

**Left:** *Giacinto Facchetti tussles with Brazilian forward Jairzinho in the 1970 World Cup final*

Giacinto Facchetti started his career as a striker with local side Trevigliese but he was spotted by the manager of Internazionale, Helenio Herrera, and converted into one of the most feared attacking defenders of his generation. He won four Scudetti (league titles) and five cups in his first eight years in Milan, and was selected for the national team in 1963 on the back of his outstanding club form.

He played at the 1966 World Cup but the tournament was a disappointment and Italy were eliminated at the group stage after defeats to the Soviet Union and North Korea. Two years later, much of the same side won the European Championships, and they then built on this success by reaching the final of the 1970 World Cup in Mexico. The Italians didn't concede a goal until the knockout phase, where they saw off the hosts (4-1) and then West Germany 4-3 in one of the best matches in World Cup history.

The final against Brazil was billed as the world's best defence against the game's best attack and for the first hour the two cancelled one another out. The Brazilians burst into life in the last quarter of the match, however, and the tiring Italians faded to lose 4-1. Facchetti also appeared at the 1974 World Cup and he eventually retired from international football three years later. He played his entire senior career with Inter, racking up 629 appearances and 75 goals, remarkable figures for a defender. He managed several clubs in later life, including his beloved Inter, but he died of cancer in 2006. The club immediately retired the number three jersey.

---

**Name:** Giacinto Facchetti
**Born:** July 18th 1942, Treviglio, Italy
**Died:** September 4th 2006, Milan
**Position:** Left back
**International Career:** 1963 - 1977
**Caps:** 94
**Goals:** 3
**Honours:** European Championship Winner (1968), World Cup Runner-up (1970)

---

# Falcão

Falcão joined Internacional in his home country in 1972. In the next eight years he played 158 league games, scored 22 goals and won three national championships (1975, 1976 and 1979). A big-money move to Roma followed where he was even better, scoring another 22 league goals in 107 games. They would have won the 1980/81 Scudetto had Roma not had a goal ruled out against Juventus but Falcão had to make do with the Coppa Italia instead.

He inexplicably missed out on selection for the 1978 World Cup, but by 1982 he was one of the finest midfielders in the world and could not be ignored for the World Cup in Spain. His goals were vital in Brazil's matches against the Soviet Union and New Zealand, and he then helped them overcome archrivals Argentina. Despite only needing a draw against Italy to progress to the semi-final, Paulo Rossi's unforgettable hat-trick meant that Falcão was a devastated member of one of the best teams never to have won the tournament. In fact he was so distressed after the match – in which he had scored the second equaliser only for Rossi to score a late winner – that he vowed to retire.

He was past his best at the 1986 World Cup in Mexico and had probably been picked on reputation and ability rather than form. He only played in two of the matches (as a sub against Spain and Algeria) and he retired after Brazil's exit to a Platini-inspired France in the quarter-final. Indeed he, Liam Brady and Platini were the three big foreign stars in Serie A for the next four years, although Falcão left Europe after an unauthorised knee operation and returned to Brazil to coach. He briefly took the reins of the national team after the 1990 World Cup but he achieved little and retired after managing Japan for a year in 1994. He returned to management in 2011 with Internacional, however.

| | |
|---|---|
| **Name:** | (Paulo Roberto) Falcão |
| **Born:** | October 16th 1953, Abelardo Luz, Brazil |
| **Position:** | Midfield |
| **International Career:** | 1976 – 1986 |
| **Caps:** | 34 |
| **Goals:** | 7 |
| **Honours:** | World Cup Squad (1982, 1986) |

# Fontaine

Just Fontaine played for Casablanca in his home country for the first three years of his career. In just 48 league appearances he scored 62 goals, and was snapped up by Nice in France. He couldn't quite match his scoring record at Casablanca but Stade Reims saw enough promise to recruit him in 1956. Although he'd first represented France in 1953, he didn't play every game for the national side. Another 122 goals in 131 league starts saw him selected for the 1958 World Cup in Sweden, however.

Fontaine delivered in every match, scoring a hat-trick against Paraguay, a brace against Yugoslavia (in a losing cause), and another goal against Scotland. He was on target again in the knockout phase, scoring twice against Northern Ireland and once against Brazil in the semi-final, a match in which a young Pelé scored three to take the South Americans to the final. Sweden beat West Germany in the second semi but Fontaine smashed four past the Germans in the third-place playoff.

His 13 World Cup goals puts him fourth on the all-time list behind Ronaldo (15), Gerd Müller (14) and Miroslav Klose (14) but Fontaine scored his at a single tournament, which remains a record. Müller and Klose needed two World Cups, while Ronaldo took four to reach 15 goals.

Had Fontaine not been forced to retire through injury at the relatively young age of 28, he would surely have smashed more records and be mentioned in the same breath as Pelé, Cruyff and Maradona.

---

**Name:** Just Fontaine
**Born:** August 18th 1933, Marrakech, Morocco
**Position:** Striker
**International Career:** 1953 - 1960
**Caps:** 21
**Goals:** 30
**Honours:** World Cup Third Place and Golden Boot (1958)

---

# Francescoli

Francescoli began his career in Montevideo but then moved to River Plate, where he scored a goal every two games for four years. He came to Europe in 1986 and continued his terrific form with RC Paris and then Olympique Marseille. He then enjoyed five seasons in Italy before rejoining River Plate to see out his career.

It was with the national side that he became known to a wider audience however. He missed out on the 1982 World Cup in Spain but played at the next two tournaments at a time when Uruguay were one of the strongest South American sides: they won the Copa América in 1983, 1987 and 1995 with Francescoli in the engine room.

He moved with a fluidity and grace that earned him the nickname 'The Prince', and there's no doubt that players like Zinedine Zidane tried to emulate his technique. Pelé named him as one of the greatest living footballers in 2004 and, eight years later, at the age of 50, he scored a bicycle kick during Ariel Ortega's testimonial, one of four goals he netted in the match. He ended his career with 645 appearances and 237 goals.

**Name:** Enzo Francescoli Uriarte
**Born:** November 12th 1961, Montevideo, Uruguay
**Position:** Attacking midfielder
**International Career:** 1982 – 1997
**Caps:** 73
**Goals:** 17
**Honours:** World Cup Round of 16 (1986, 1990)

# Garrincha

Garrincha was born with severe birth defects – a curved spine, twisted right leg and a left leg six centimetres shorter and curved outwards – to an alcoholic father, but he was determined to make it as a professional footballer. He was married and with a child before he had a trial with Botafogo, however. He was such a technically gifted player that Nílton Santos insisted the club hire him and he also put him forward for the national team. Garrincha scored a hat-trick on his professional debut but couldn't break into the Brazilian team for the 1954 World Cup because the selectors went with Julinho. His club career would go from strength to strength however: over the next 12 years he made 581 appearances for Botafogo and scored 232 goals.

He was picked for the 1958 World Cup in Sweden on the back of his outstanding form and he repeatedly terrorised defenders with his pace and skill. His career then took a bizarre turn: he was dropped for a friendly against England because of his drinking, then he got a local girl pregnant when touring in Sweden, and when he returned home he ran his father over while both were drunk. His father died in 1959 from liver cancer.

When Pelé was injured during the 1962 World Cup, Garrincha picked up the baton and guided the team to the final. He was voted player of the tournament after a 3-1 win over Czechoslovakia. He played his last international match against Hungary during the 1966 World Cup. It was the only match Brazil lost while he was playing.

His personal life was in stark contrast to his glittering football career. He was involved in many road accidents, one of which killed his mother-in-law, and he fathered at least 14 children by four women. He died a forgotten hero in 1983 after being hospitalised eight times with severe alcoholism. He was then voted one of the three greatest forwards of the 20th century.

**Above:** *Garrincha, 'The Little Bird', was one of the most influential Brazilian players of the 1950s and '60s*

| | |
|---|---|
| **Name:** | Garrincha (Manuel Francisco dos Santos) |
| **Born:** | October 28th 1933, Pau Grande, Brazil |
| **Died:** | January 20th 1983, Rio de Janeiro |
| **Position:** | Wing |
| **International Career:** | 1955 - 1966 |
| **Caps:** | 50 |
| **Goals:** | 12 |
| **Honours:** | World Cup Winner (1958, 1962) |

# Gerrard

Steven Gerrard began his career with Whiston Juniors before being spotted by Liverpool scouts and joining the youth academy at the age of nine. He eventually signed for the club in 1997 but had to wait more than a year to make his first-team debut. His nerves and initial lack of ability meant he didn't make much of an impact but Liverpool stuck by him and played him alongside Jamie Redknapp in the midfield. He then overcame several serious injuries to cement his place in the team.

Gerrard made his international debut against Ukraine in 2000 but he only made a substitute's appearance at the following European Championships. His first England goal was a magnificent 30-yard strike against Germany in Munich in 2001, which helped ensure the side's qualification for the 2002 World Cup (albeit via a playoff match against Greece). He pulled out of the squad with an injury but played well enough at Euro 2004 to reach his first World Cup two years later.

He scored two goals but then saw his penalty saved in the shootout against Portugal in the quarter-final. The qualifying campaign for Euro 2008 was equally disappointing and Gerrard had to wait until 2010 to perform again on the world stage. England were expected to do well in South Africa but they were clearly a league below the Germans and lost 4-1.

Roy Hodgson named Gerrard as his captain during the qualifying campaign for Euro 2012 and Gerrard was on superb form at the tournament. He supplied three killer passes in England's group games and was named man-of-the-match against co-hosts Ukraine. Although they went out to Italy on penalties in the knockout phase, Gerrard was the only English player named in the team of the tournament.

Gerrard's long-range passing and devastating shot have singled him out as the finest midfielder of his generation. Sir Alex Ferguson's tongue must have

been firmly in his cheek when he said he didn't believe Gerrard was amongst the world's best as the Liverpool midfielder remains the only man to have scored in a League Cup final, FA Cup final, UEFA Cup final and the Champions League final. Indeed, when Liverpool were 3-0 down to AC Milan in the latter match in 2005, Gerrard single-handedly inspired the fight-back that saw the Merseysiders score three and then take the game on penalties. And the standard of football in the Champions League is arguably higher than at the European Championships or the World Cup.

**Name:** Steven George Gerrard MBE
**Born:** May 30th 1980, Whiston, England
**Position:** Midfielder
**International Career:** 2000 - present
**Caps:** 108
**Goals:** 21
**Honours:** Champions League Winner (2005)

# Gérson

Gérson's father and uncle were professional footballers, and his heroes as a boy were Zizinho, Ademir and Danilo. He was a player of some talent and signed for Flamengo in 1959. In the next four years he played 153 league matches and scored 80 goals, most of which were with his devastating left foot. He had the ability to read and control the game from midfield and he was soon called up to the national team. Were it not for a serious knee injury, he would surely have partnered Garrincha, Pelé and Didi to World Cup glory in Chile in 1962. Four years later he had a poor tournament in England but he was at his peak for Mexico '70.

As one of the greatest passers and tacticians, Gérson masterminded Brazil's victory and he scored in the final against Italy. He was the standout player in the tournament so it came as something of a surprise when Pelé overlooked him in his list of 125 greatest living footballers in 2004. His 14 goals in 70 Brazilian starts and 207 goals in 603 games overall suggest he was easily good enough to make the grade.

**Name:** Gérson (de Oliveira Nunes)
**Born:** January 11th 1941, Niterói, Brazil
**Position:** Playmaker
**International Career:** 1961 – 1972
**Caps:** 70
**Goals:** 14
**Honours:** World Cup Winner (1970)

# Gullit

One of the most versatile players to grace the game, Gullit was an inspirational captain who led the Netherlands to victory in the 1988 European Championships. He enjoyed success with the top clubs in Holland, Italy and England before turning his considerable talents to management.

Born Ruud Dil in a poor area of Amsterdam in September 1962, he played street football throughout his youth with the likes of Frank Rijkaard. He was soon spotted by the DWS club and he then made it into the Dutch youth team alongside the Koeman brothers and Wim Kieft. As a precociously talented teenager he made his debut for HFC Haarlem and was named the best player in the division. Several English clubs turned him down so he moved to Feyenoord in 1982 and ended up playing alongside the great Johan Cruyff. The following season the club secured the league and cup double and, having been named footballer of the year, he moved to domestic giants PSV, where he was also named the best player

in his first season. A big-money move to AC Milan in 1987 brought more success – the Scudetto and two European Cups – but injuries forced him to watch from the sidelines for much of the early 1990s.

Such a talent was bound to make an impression on the international stage and Gullit didn't disappoint, although his early years were characterised by poor team performances. He made his debut aged 19 in 1981 but the Netherlands repeatedly failed to qualify for the main tournaments and it wasn't until Gullit was captain that they qualified for the 1988 European Championships.

Although the Dutch lost their first match against the Soviet Union, they progressed by beating England, the Republic of Ireland and then Germany in a grudge match in Hamburg. The final was a rematch against the Russians but a close-range Gullit header and a magical Van Basten volley secured the trophy for the Dutch, their first international silverware. Although touted as potential champions of the world at Italia '90,

# GULLIT

new national coach Dick Advocaat led to Gullit's retirement from international football in 1994.

He then moved to England, becoming one of the first international stars to grace the Premiership. The likes of Gianfranco Zola, Dennis Bergkamp and Eric Cantona soon followed. Gullit seemed happiest in London and he took the player/manager role at Chelsea when Glen Hoddle left to take the vacant England job. They finished sixth in the league and won the FA Cup. He then enjoyed spells at Newcastle, Feyenoord and Los Angeles Galaxy before taking up a punditry position with the media.

Gullit's knee injuries and several underwhelming performances saw them lose to the Germans in another ill-tempered match in the second round. Euro '92 looked like being a strong tournament for the Dutch but they came unstuck against an inspired Denmark in the semi-final and went out on penalties. Frequent altercations with

**Name:** Ruud Gullit
**Born:** September 1st 1962, Amsterdam, Netherlands
**Position:** Midfield
**International Career:** 1981 - 1994
**Caps:** 66
**Goals:** 17
**Honours:** European Championship Winner (1988)

# Hagi

Gheorghe Hagi started his career with Farul Constanta in 1978, and he was immediately noticed by the manager of Luceafãrul Bucuresti. He played with the latter for a season before rejoining the youth club but it wasn't long before he found himself with domestic giants Steaua Bucuresti. Big-money moves to Real Madrid and Barcelona followed but he ended his club career with Galatasaray in Turkey.

On the international stage, he was a revelation. He first played for his country in 1983 and was ever-present until his remarkable showing at USA '94. In their first group match Hagi lobbed Colombian keeper Oscar Córdoba from 40 yards to seal a 3-1 win, but then they were surprisingly humiliated by Switzerland, 4-1. Hagi's side bounced back to defeat the hosts at the Pasadena Rose Bowl and progress top of their group. Hagi was on target again when Romania shocked Argentina 3-2 in the round of 16 but the side then lost a penalty shootout to Sweden after the match finished 2-2.

Hagi had promised to retire after the 1998 World Cup in France but Romania's strong showing in the group saw him change his mind. They beat Colombia 1-0 and a solid England 2-1 before drawing their last match with Tunisia. They progressed as group winners before losing to Croatia in the knockout stages. Hagi returned in time for the 2000 European Championships but he was sent off in Romania's quarter-final loss to Italy, a sad end to a glittering domestic and international career. He moved into management in 2001 and flitted between several clubs, but he was sacked from Galatasaray in 2011 after a string of poor results and hasn't worked in football since.

**Above:**
*Romania's Gheorghe Hagi celebrates another wonder goal*

| | |
|---|---|
| **Name:** | Gheorghe Hagi |
| **Born:** | February 5th 1965, Sãcele, Romania |
| **Position:** | Attacking midfielder |
| **International Career:** | 1983 – 2000 |
| **Caps:** | 125 |
| **Goals:** | 35 |
| **Honours:** | FIFA World Cup All-Star Team (1994) |

# Henry

Having had a disappointing 1998-9 season at Juventus, Henry moved to Arsenal and swapped his usual wing position for striker. It proved to be a shrewd buy by Arsène Wenger and an inspired tactical move as Henry, a man blessed with exceptional skill, devastating pace and a fierce shot, soon became the most feared front-man in the Premier League. He was also a top-class finisher for France, helping them to the 1998 World Cup and the European Championship trophy in 2000.

Thierry Daniel Henry was born in Paris in 1977. Having not shown much interest in the sport, his father persuaded him to take it more seriously and he showed promise as a schoolboy while playing for local club side CO Les Ulis. He was then snapped up by AS Monaco as a 13-year-old after scoring all six goals in a lower-league match. The club insisted he complete an academic course before manager Arsène Wenger gave him his debut, which he subsequently made on the wing in 1994.

Monaco won the 1996-7 league title and, the following year, Henry scored seven goals on their way to the Champions League semi-final. Despite not being completely happy on the wing, he was handed his international debut before the 1998 World Cup and he was an integral part of the side that dominated the tournament. A big-money move to Italian giants Juventus did not go according to plan so Henry followed Wenger to Arsenal.

It was in North London that Henry finally realised his potential. Despite a slow start – he took his time developing into a striker – he helped Arsenal to second place in the league and the final of the 1999 UEFA Cup. On the international front, Henry was the focal point of a team that destroyed the competition and took the European Championship. Domestically, Arsenal finally delivered the success he craved in 2001-2 when they secured the league and cup double but France were the surprise casualties from their group at the 2002 World Cup.

Henry's club form didn't suffer from the ignominy of the early exit and he came second in the 2003 World Player of the Year poll. He delivered again the following season and, along with the likes of Dennis Bergkamp and Patrick Vieira, he helped the Gunners go unbeaten throughout the entire league season, the first time this had been achieved in more than 100 years.

He broke more records in 2006 when he surpassed Ian Wright and Cliff Bastin's goal-scoring milestones, although Arsenal couldn't edge past Barcelona in the Champions League final. Henry played well at the World Cup in Germany but couldn't help his side overcome Italy in the final. On the domestic front, he joined the Catalans after the tournament and guided them to the Copa del Rey, the league title and the Champions League for a unique treble. Having returned from the disastrous World Cup in South Africa, where his team-mates went on strike and refused to train after Nicolas Anelka was sent home, Henry announced his international retirement and was sold to the New York Red Bulls.

**Above:** *Thierry Henry of France in action during the international friendly match between France and Poland*

**Name:** Thierry Daniel Henry
**Born:** August 17th 1977, Paris, France
**Position:** Forward
**International Career:** 1997 - 2010
**Caps:** 123
**Goals:** 51
**Honours:** World Cup Winner (1998), European Championship Winner (2000), World Cup Runner-up (2006)

# Hidegkuti

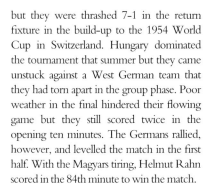

Nándor Hidegkuti began his career with Elektromos in 1942, and he then joined MTK Hungária at the end of the war. In his first four seasons he scored 73 league goals in 110 appearances and earned a call-up to the national team. He was one of a golden generation of Hungarian players who steamrolled their way to the peak of world football with a mix of brilliance (32 consecutive matches unbeaten before the 1954 World Cup final) and brutality (the infamous World Cup quarter-final against Brazil in Bern).

It is for the former that the side should be remembered, however. Alongside Puskás, Czibor and Kocsis, Hidegkuti was simply irresistible: he scored two goals on debut against Romania, a hat-trick against Bulgaria in his second international, and a hat-trick against England at Wembley in a 6-3 demolition of the self-proclaimed best team in the world. Playing in a central position behind the striker but with a licence to attack, opposing teams simply couldn't hope with his positional awareness, skill and pace. England should have learned from their mistakes

but they were thrashed 7-1 in the return fixture in the build-up to the 1954 World Cup in Switzerland. Hungary dominated the tournament that summer but they came unstuck against a West German team that they had torn apart in the group phase. Poor weather in the final hindered their flowing game but they still scored twice in the opening ten minutes. The Germans rallied, however, and levelled the match in the first half. With the Magyars tiring, Helmut Rahn scored in the 84th minute to win the match.

Hungary were a team in decline by the 1958 World Cup and they lost a playoff match against Wales that meant they didn't make it out of their group. Hidegkuti retired and moved into management the following year. The highlight of his coaching career was leading ACF Fiorentina to the Cup Winners' Cup in 1961. He died of heart and lung problems in 2002.

**Name:** Nándor Hidegkuti
**Born:** March 3rd 1922, Budapest, Hungary
**Died:** February 14th 2002, Budapest
**Position:** Inside forward
**International Career:** 1945 – 1958
**Caps:** 69
**Goals:** 39
**Honours:** Olympic Gold Medal (1952), World Cup Runner-up (1954)

# Hurst

Geoff Hurst's father played for Bristol Rovers and Oldham Athletic so young Geoff had football in the blood. He played one first-class cricket match but scored nought in both innings and decided to concentrate on football instead. He joined West Ham as a youth and turned professional in 1959.

He endured a slow start to his career and considered returning to cricket but Ron Greenwood convinced him otherwise, playing him up front alongside Johnny Byrne so his defensive frailties weren't exploited. The two formed a steady partnership and Hurst scored the winner in the 1964 FA Cup semi-final against Manchester United. West Ham came from behind twice against Preston North End to win the trophy at Wembley and Hurst was suddenly in frame for the national team. The following year the side won the Cup Winners' Cup.

Hurst made his international debut against West Germany in the build-up to the 1966 World Cup. He played well enough in the next two warm-up games to secure a place in Alf Ramsey's squad but Jimmy Greaves was the top striker and Hurst had to make do with a place on the bench for the group games against Mexico, Uruguay and France. England progressed but Greaves picked up a nasty cut in the France game and Hurst scored the winner against Argentina in the quarter-final. He then set up Bobby Charlton for the winner against Portugal in the semi.

Greaves was fit again for the final but Ramsey defied the press and every armchair pundit by sticking with Hurst for the showdown against West Germany. Hurst repaid the faith by scoring the first – and so far only – hat-trick in a World Cup final as England won 4-2. His second goal remains the most hotly disputed in football history as it rebounded from the underside of the crossbar and landed close to the goal line. The linesman awarded the goal, which gave England a 3-2 lead. He completed the historic hat-trick with a thunderous shot in the last minute.

**Above:** *Geoff Hurst*

Hurst was in the squad for the World Cup defence in Mexico four years later but, despite taking a 2-0 lead against West Germany in the quarter-final, they capitulated in the heat and the Germans avenged their Wembley defeat with three late goals. After picking up an injury in 1972, he retired from international football.

**Name:** Sir Geoffrey Charles 'Geoff' Hurst MBE
**Born:** December 8th 1941, Lancashire, England
**Position:** Striker
**International Career:** 1966 - 1972
**Caps:** 49
**Goals:** 24
**Honours:** World Cup Winner (1966)

# Inamoto

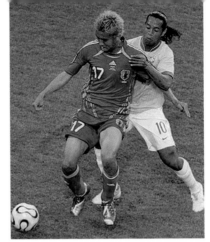

Junichi Inamoto enjoyed five years in the Gamba Osaka youth team before making the senior squad in 1997. He gained a reputation as a tough-tackling midfielder with an eye for the odd spectacular goal and he was called up by Japan in time for the 2000 Asian Cup, which his side won.

Inamoto put Japan 2-1 up against Belgium in their first group match at the 2002 World Cup on home soil, but a late Van der Heyden strike secured a draw for the Belgians. Inamoto scored again to beat Russia, and Japan qualified top of their group with another win over Tunisia. Sadly the co-hosts were eliminated in the knockout phase by Turkey. Four years later in Germany, Japan failed to qualify from a tough group that included Brazil, Australia and Croatia.

Japan qualified for the 2010 World Cup in South Africa but Inamoto only came on as a late substitute in their 1-0 victory over Cameroon. He didn't play against the Netherlands and was again used as a sub in a 3-1 win over Denmark that saw them through to the knockout phase. Japan were then beaten by Paraguay on penalties. Inamoto had shown that he could play at the highest level, however, and his domestic career included stints at Arsenal, Fulham and Galatasaray. He is now with Kawasaki Frontale in his home country, and he may yet play a role at the 2014 World Cup in Brazil.

**Name:** Junichi Inamoto
**Born:** September 18th 1979, Kagoshima, Japan
**Position:** Midfield
**International Career:** 2000 – present
**Caps:** 82
**Goals:** 5
**Honours:** World Cup Round of 16 (2002, 2010)

# Jairzinho

**Below:** *Jairzinho at the 1974 World Cup*

Jairzinho joined youth side Botafogo and made his professional debut for the senior team at the age of 15. He couldn't play in his preferred position initially because Garrincha played on the right so he switched to the left and made an immediate impact. He resisted the temptation to move to Europe and spent 15 glorious years with Botafogo, making 413 league appearances and scoring 186 goals, an incredible return for a midfielder, albeit one who bombed forward at every opportunity to whip in devilish crosses or to shoot.

He made his debut for the national team when Garrincha was injured in 1964, but he couldn't help the side past the opening round at the 1966 World Cup in England. When Garrincha retired, Jairzinho switched back to the right and became the legendary 'Hurricane' at the 1970 World Cup in Mexico. He scored in every match of the tournament, one of only three players ever to do so (the others being Uruguay's Alcides Ghiggia in 1950 and France's Just Fontaine in 1958), although he didn't win the Golden Boot as Germany's Gerd Müller scored ten to his seven.

He scored another two goals at the 1974 World Cup but he couldn't guide the side to the final and they bowed out in the playoff for third place. Jairzinho's domestic career wound down over the same period and, although he continued for a number of clubs, he never stayed more than a season or two and finally hung up his boots after a farewell international in 1982. He returned to football 20 years later as manager of Gabon.

He continues to be revered as a player and is consistently voted one of the top 30 players of all time. He is also credited with spotting Ronaldo as a 14-year-old and recommending him to Cruzeiro. Ronaldo would go on to become one of the game's modern greats and a three-time World Player of the Year.

**Name:** Jairzinho (Jair Ventura Filho)
**Born:** December 25th 1944, Rio de Janeiro, Brazil
**Position:** Wing
**International Career:** 1964 – 1982
**Caps:** 81
**Goals:** 33
**Honours:** World Cup Winner (1970)

# Jung-Hwan

**Above:** *Ahn Jung-Hwan*

Ahn Jung-Hwan began his senior career with Pusan I'cons and scored a goal every other game in his two seasons with the club. This earned him a transfer to Italian side Perugia but his time with the Serie A side was short-lived and controversial because of an incident at the 2002 World Cup in the Far East.

South Korea were not expected to do well but the co-hosts beat Poland and Portugal to qualify for the knockout phase. In their round of 16 match against Italy, Christian Vieri put the Azzurri ahead but a late Seol Ki-Hyeon equaliser sent the game into extra time. With only three minutes left, Ahn scored the golden-goal winner. Perugia's president, Luciano Gaucci, called Ahn immediately after the match to tell him he'd cancelled his contract and he would never play for Perugia again, although he did eventually change his mind. Ahn was incensed, however, and he rejected Gaucci's offer to buy out his contract. After another controversial game against Spain, in which the referee disallowed two Spanish goals, South Korea found themselves in the semi-final of their own World Cup. Michael Ballack's Germany proved too strong, however, and South Korea also lost the third-place playoff.

Ahn had brief stints with clubs at home and abroad and he was selected for the 2006 World Cup in Germany. He came off the bench and scored the winner against Togo in the group stage, but a draw with France and a loss to Switzerland saw them eliminated. He also played at the 2010 World Cup but, having qualified from their group, South Korea were beaten in the round of 16 by Uruguay. Ahn finally retired from international football in 2012 and is widely regarded as his country's greatest player.

**Name:** Ahn Jung-Hwan
**Born:** January 27th 1976, Paju, South Korea
**Position:** Attacking midfield
**International Career:** 1997 - 2010
**Caps:** 71
**Goals:** 17
**Honours:** World Cup Fourth Place (2002)

# Kahn

Kahn started as an outfield player for local side Karlsruher SC at the age of six. He soon realized his calling lay between the sticks, however, and he spent the next 12 years honing his skills with the junior team. In 1987 he was included in the club's professional Bundesliga squad, although he was second choice behind Alexander Famulla. He made his home debut before Christmas in a 4-0 victory over FC Köln. He then had to wait another three years before cementing a place in the starting XI. He delivered a number of outstanding performances and helped the side to the semi-final of the 1993-4 UEFA Cup.

Kahn attracted the interest of several clubs but he eventually signed for Bayern Munich in 1994 for a record £1.5 million. He ruptured cruciate ligaments having only just established himself as the number one 'keeper, but he made his debut for the national squad two months after regaining his fitness. He followed that up with a UEFA Cup win and then the 1996-7 Bundesliga title and the League Cup.

He spent most of Euro '96 and France '98 on the bench but he made the national number one jersey his own after Andreas Köpke's retirement. His first major tournament was a disaster, with Germany exiting Euro 2000 at the group stage, but the 2002 World Cup cemented his reputation as the world's finest goalkeeper. Now captain, he guided a poor German side to the final against Brazil. Whereas in the earlier matches he'd been inspirational (he kept five clean sheets and only conceded one goal), in the final he was uncharacteristically fragile and Brazil won 2-0. Nevertheless, Kahn was named the tournament's best player and received the Golden Ball.

Germany were again poor at Euro 2004 and Kahn handed the captaincy to Michael Ballack. When Jürgen Klinsmann took over as coach before the 2006 World Cup, he rotated Kahn and Jens Lehmann, with the latter being preferred for the tournament.

Kahn took the disappointment well and agreed to warm the bench. Germany were eliminated in the semi-final by Italy so Kahn was drafted in for the third-place playoff, which Germany won 3-1 against Portugal. It was the Titan's last international match. He will be remembered as a formidable shot-stopper with great presence and handling.

**Name:** Oliver Rolf Kahn
**Born:** June 15th 1969, Karlsruhe, Germany
**Position:** Goalkeeper
**International Career:** 1995 - 2006
**Caps:** 86
**Goals:** 0
**Honours:** European Championship Winner (1996), World Cup Runner-up (2002)

**Above:** *Oliver Kahn's testimonial match in Munich in 2008*

# Kempes

**Right:** *Mario Kempes celebrates scoring against the Dutch in the 1978 World Cup final*

**M**ario Kempes began his career at the age of 16 with Instituto. A move to Rosario Central saw him score 85 league goals in only 107 matches, and this attracted the attention of Valencia. He helped the Spanish side to three cups and was top scorer in La Liga in the two seasons leading up to the 1978 World Cup.

National coach César Luis Menotti selected him despite the fact that he was the only Argentinean playing abroad, but the gamble appeared to be misguided when Kempes failed to score in the first group stage of the tournament. Argentina managed to beat Hungary and France, and they progressed to the second phase despite losing 1-0 to Italy.

Thereafter, however, Kempes was a revelation: he scored twice against Poland (although he should have been sent off for a deliberate handball on the line); twice more against Peru in the 6-0 drubbing that saw Brazil controversially knocked out on goal difference; and twice again in the final against the Dutch. His six goals saw him win the Golden Boot.

He failed to score an international goal in the next four years and by the 1982 World Cup he was overshadowed by the emerging talent that was Maradona. Kempes's international career was therefore over by the age of 27. He moved into management in 1996 but he didn't enjoy much success and now commentates for the Spanish arm of ESPN.

**Name:** Mario Alberto Kempes (Chiodi)
**Born:** July 15th 1954, Belle Ville, Argentina
**Position:** Striker
**International Career:** 1973 - 1982
**Caps:** 43
**Goals:** 20
**Honours:** World Cup Winner (1978)

# Klinsmann

Jürgen Klinsmann began playing for local side TB Gingen at the age of eight. In a single match later in the season, he scored 16 goals and by the time he was 16 he'd signed for Stuttgarter Kickers, where he would begin his professional career. In 1984 he joined VfB Stuttgart and was soon the top scorer in the Bundesliga. In 1987 he was capped by his country against Brazil, and the following season he was German footballer of the year. He then joined Italian giants Inter alongside compatriots Lothar Matthäus and Andreas Brehme.

At Italia '90 Klinsmann was outstanding. West Germany topped their group after wins over Yugoslavia and the UAE. This meant they faced the Dutch in the round of 16 in an epic encounter that defined the intense and bitter rivalry between the nations. Rudi Völler and Frank Rijkaard were both sent off, with the latter then spitting at Völler as they walked off. With the match threatening to boil over, Klinsmann put the Germans ahead and Brehme added a second before

Ronald Koeman scored a consolation penalty late on.

The West Germans saw off Czechoslovakia and then England after another epic game in Turin. The final against Argentina was a dour affair that saw the South Americans reduced to nine men after persistent fouling. Brehme scored a penalty in the 85th minute to seal the win.

Germany were expected to do well at Euro '92 but this time they lost a dull final to Denmark. Despite scoring five goals at USA '94, Klinsmann's Germany were again beaten by underdogs in the shape of Bulgaria. He was integral once more during Euro '96 in England when Germany won the trophy at Wembley, and he scored another three goals at the 1998 World Cup in France. The Germans eventually lost 3-0 to Croatia in the quarter-final and Klinsmann retired.

He moved into coaching with the national team in 2004 but his overtly offensive style was criticised as many players neglected their defensive duties. Fans

**Above:** *Jürgen Klinsmann celebrates his superb goal at the 1994 World Cup in the USA*

and critics were won over by Germany's performance at the 2006 World Cup, however. They won their group games and also defeated Sweden and Argentina, although they then lost the semi-final against Italy. Klinsmann is currently the head coach of the US national team, and he guided the side to World Cup qualification for Brazil in 2014.

**Name:** Jürgen Klinsmann
**Born:** July 30th 1964, Göppingen, West Germany
**Position:** Striker
**International Career:** 1987 - 1998
**Caps:** 108
**Goals:** 47
**Honours:** World Cup Winner (1990), European Championship Winner (1996)

# Kocsis

Sándor Kocsis was a goal-scoring machine who surely ranks as one of the finest marksmen the game has seen. He graduated from youth side Kobanyai TC to Ferencváros TC and promptly won the 1949 league title. During his national service he joined the army team Honvéd alongside the likes of Jósef Bozsik, Zoltán Czibor and the legendary Ferenc Puskás. Over the next three years he broke scoring records for fun and became an integral player in Hungary's golden generation, which also included Nándor Hidegkuti.

Having first been selected for the national team in 1948, the side then went unbeaten for 32 games between June 1950 and the 1954 World Cup final. He scored hat-tricks against Sweden, Finland and Czechoslovakia before helping to dismantle England 6-3 at Wembley and 7-1 in Budapest, shattering the illusion that the country gave the sport to the world was still a force on the international stage.

Kocsis was sensational at the 1954 World Cup: he scored two more hat-tricks and finished the tournament as the top scorer with 11. Two of those came in the infamous Battle of Bern, a particularly violent match against Brazil that Hungary eventually won 4-2. Kocsis contributed another two goals to see off defending champions Uruguay in the semi-final. This set up another match against West Germany, against whom Kocsis had scored four in the second game of the tournament.

Hungary had the highest ranking of any football team in history and they were expected to thrash the Germans again. The match was played in appalling conditions but that didn't stop an injured Puskás putting Hungary ahead after six minutes. When Czibor scored a second two minutes later, the pundits and bookmakers thought they'd got things right.

But German coach Sepp Herberger had fielded a weakened side in the earlier group match, his team were playing with the latest Adidas boots and the weather favoured their style of football. Ten minutes later they were level after Max Morlock and Helmut Rahn both scored,

**Right:** *The legendary Hungarian Sándor Kocsis*

although it later emerged that the German players had probably been given illegal stimulants to help them get through the match.

Kocsis played on for the national team for two more years and domestically until 1966, by which time he'd accumulated seven international hat-tricks, the best goals-per-game ratio of any player with more than 45 caps, and more than 400 domestic goals in total. His coaching career was curtailed by a diagnosis of leukaemia and stomach cancer, and he fell to his death from the fourth floor of a hospital in Barcelona in 1979.

but the magnificent Magyars weren't swayed from launching wave after wave of attacks. However, German goalkeeper Toni Turek wouldn't be beaten again and Rahn scored the winner six minutes from time. Puskás thought he'd levelled in the dying moments but it was ruled offside and West Germany held on to win the World Cup. The Miracle of Bern remains one of the biggest upsets in sporting history,

**Name:** Sándor Kocsis (Péter)
**Born:** September 21st 1929, Budapest, Hungary
**Died:** July 22nd 1979, Barcelona, Spain
**Position:** Forward
**International Career:** 1948 – 1956
**Caps:** 68
**Goals:** 75
**Honours:** Olympic Gold Medal (1952), World Cup Runner-up (1954)

# Kopaszewski

Raymond Kopa was born to a family of Polish immigrants. He joined Angers in the second tier of French football in 1949 and scored 15 goals over the next three seasons from midfield. He then had six productive years with Stade Reims before being lured to Real Madrid by Alfredo di Stéfano. When Ferenc Puskás joined the side, Real became the dominant domestic force in Europe, and Kopa was an integral part of the side that won another three consecutive European Cups and two league titles. He returned to Reims in 1959 and remained there for another eight years.

Kopa made his international debut in 1952 and scored against Mexico at the 1954 World Cup but it wasn't until four years later in Sweden that the wider world was treated to his skill in marshalling the midfield. He scored against Paraguay and Scotland but was powerless to stop the Pelé-inspired Brazilians in the semi-final. He scored again in the playoff against West Germany to finish the tournament with three goals, but it was his assists for

Just Fontaine that set him apart.

Kopa retired from international football after France failed to qualify for the 1962 World Cup. In 1970 he became the first footballer to be awarded the Légion d'honneur, the highest decoration in France.

*Left:* France's Raymond Kopa

---

**Name:** Raymond 'Kopa' Kopaszewski
**Born:** October 13th 1931, Nœux-les-Mines, France
**Position:** Attacking midfield
**International Career:** 1952 – 1962
**Caps:** 45
**Goals:** 18
**Honours:** World Cup Third Place (1958)

---

# Krankl

Hans Krankl joined Rapid Wien as a 17-year-old and he remained with the club for eight years, scoring 160 league goals in 205 starts. He signed for Barcelona in 1978 and enjoyed three successful years in Spain, winning the Copa del Rey, the Cup Winners' Cup and the Golden Boot for being the top scorer in the league. He then returned to Rapid for six more seasons, scoring another 107 goals.

Such was his talent that he was selected for the Austrian national team aged only 20 but he missed out on the following year's World Cup. In 1978, however, he was one of the best strikers in the world. He scored against Spain and Sweden, and Austria topped their group above Brazil. They were uncharacteristically poor in a 5-1 hammering by the Dutch in the second round, and they then narrowly lost to Italy. In a cracking match against West Germany, Krankl netted twice and dumped their illustrious neighbours out of the tournament but Austria were also out having finished bottom of the group.

Both sides qualified for the knockout phase of the 1982 World Cup in Spain. Austria beat Chile and Algeria (with Krankl on the score-sheet) but lost to West Germany. They couldn't progress from the second phase but Krankl played on for the national team for another three years. When he retired from domestic football in 1989 he'd scored more than 450 senior goals, and he has since been recognised as the finest Austrian footballer of all time.

**Name:** Johann 'Hans' Krankl
**Born:** February 14th 1953, Vienna, Austria
**Position:** Striker
**International Career:** 1973 - 1985
**Caps:** 69
**Goals:** 34
**Honours:** European Golden Shoe (1978)

# Krol

Rudi Krol began his club career at Ajax under legendary coach Rinus Michels. By the age of 20 he'd cemented his place in the defence and had also been selected for his country. As a versatile player who became a key component of the Dutch total football, Krol often found himself breaking from midfield to support Cruyff and the strikers. At the 1974 World Cup in Germany he was superb: he scored a long-range thunderbolt against Argentina and supplied the pass for Cruyff to knock out the Brazilians. In the final against the hosts, the Netherlands took the lead before the opposition had even touched the ball, but the West Germans rallied and somehow overcame the superior Dutch 2-1.

Despite the departure of Cruyff, the Dutch were still a formidable outfit when they travelled to Argentina for the 1978 World Cup. Krol was now in the sweeper's role and had taken over the captaincy, and he led the side to comfortable wins over Iran, Austria and Italy, although they did suffer a shock defeat to Scotland in the group stage. The final against the hosts was locked at 1-1 when Rob Rensenbrink saw an effort rebound off the post in the last minute of normal time. The Dutch let their heads drop and Argentina scored twice in extra time to condemn the Netherlands to defeats in successive World Cup finals.

Krol led the side at the 1980 European Championships but they were eliminated in the first round. They then failed to qualify for the 1982 World Cup in Spain. Krol played his last match during the qualifying campaign for Euro '84. He went on to have a successful managerial career with a number of African clubs as well as with Ajax.

**Name:** Rudolf 'Ruud' Jozef Krol
**Born:** March 24th 1949, Amsterdam, Netherlands
**Position:** Defender
**International Career:** 1969 - 1983
**Caps:** 83
**Goals:** 4
**Honours:** World Cup Runner-up (1974, 1978)

# Larsson

LARSSON

**Right:** *Henrik Larsson takes a free-kick against the Dutch at Euro 2004*

Henrik Larsson began playing with local side Högaborg when he was only six, and he graduated to the senior side while he was still at school. In his first season with Helsingborg, he scored 34 goals and helped the side to promotion to the top flight. In their second season, the side finished mid-table and Larsson was called up to the national team.

He scored on his international debut against Finland and played a minor role for the team at the World Cup in 1994. He scored in the third-place playoff against Bulgaria to help Sweden to their best finish since losing to Brazil in the final of the 1958 World Cup. The Swedes were poor in their qualifying campaigns for Euro '96 and France '98, but they did make it to Euro 2000. Larsson scored against Italy but Sweden were eliminated at the group stage.

Larsson scored both goals against Nigeria at the 2002 World Cup to seal qualification from a tough group, and he scored again in the knockout phase against Senegal but the African side went through with a Golden Goal. He briefly retired from international football but his sensational form with Celtic (174 league goals in 221 starts) convinced him he could still perform at the highest level. His diving header against Bulgaria was voted the best goal at Euro 2004 and his pairing with Zlatan Ibrahimovic looked like developing into one of the most feared strike partnerships in the world.

Although Sweden were knocked out by the Dutch, Larsson was picked for the 2006 World Cup and, when he scored against England, he became only the sixth player to score at three tournaments. He retired afterwards but made another comeback for Euro 2008. He played his 100th international match later that year and hung up his boots for good in 2009.

**Name:** Henrik Edward Larsson
**Born:** September 20th 1971, Helsingborg, Sweden
**Position:** Striker
**International Career:** 1993 – 2009
**Caps:** 106
**Goals:** 37
**Honours:** World Cup Third Place (1994)

# Lato

It's no coincidence that Polish football enjoyed a golden era when Lato was playing for the national side. He spent the majority of his domestic career with Stal Mielec, where he scored 111 goals in 272 appearances. Polish league rules meant that he couldn't move abroad until he was 30, so the traditional European giants missed out on his best years.

He was selected for his country just before the Munich Olympics and he helped the side win the gold medal (he would win silver at Montreal four years later). He built on this success at the 1974 World Cup in Germany. He scored twice in a 3-2 win over Argentina and twice more in a 7-0 demolition of Haiti. He chipped in with winning goals against Sweden and Yugoslavia in the second phase but Poland were eventually beaten by West Germany. Lato scored the only goal in the third-place playoff against Brazil to continue a wonderful decade for Polish football.

Lato was on target again at the 1978 World Cup in Argentina, with goals against Tunisia and Brazil, but Poland went out in the second round. Four years later, Lato's goal against Peru saw Poland top their group at Spain '82. They then beat Belgium in the second phase before losing to Italy in the semi-final. Lato collected another bronze medal when the Poles defeated France 3-2 in the playoff.

He turned down an offer from Pelé to play in North America and retired from international football in 1984 with 45 goals from 104 caps. He was the complete team player with dazzling acceleration and a fierce shot with either foot. After an 11-year coaching career he moved into politics and was elected President of the Polish FA in 2008.

**Above:** *Lato evades the Brazilian defence and helps Poland to third place at the 1974 World Cup*

---

**Name:** Grzegorz Boleslaw Lato
**Born:** April 8th 1950, Malbork, Poland
**Position:** Wing
**International Career:** 1971 - 1984
**Caps:** 104
**Goals:** 45
**Honours:** Olympic Gold Medal (1972), World Cup Third Place (1974, 1982)

---

# Laudrup

Michael Laudrup began his football career with his father's youth team, Vanløse. Finn Laudrup then joined Brøndby as player/manager so his other son, Brian, also joined the side. By 1976, Brian was still with Brøndby but Michael was deemed good enough to join top-flight club Københavns Boldklub, for whom he made his debut aged 17. He then helped Brøndby to promotion and made his international debut in 1982.

The prodigiously talented youngster was soon snapped up by Lazio but his senior career didn't take off until he joined Juventus in 1985. He scored 16 goals in 102 league appearances for the Italian giants before a big-money move to Barcelona. He helped Johan Cruyff's Catalan dream team win four consecutive league titles, four cups and the European Cup in 1992 but Cruyff inexplicably left him out of the 1994 European Cup final, which Barça lost 4-0 to Milan. This snub contributed to Laudrup leaving for Madrid. He won the league in his first season with Real and helped the side crush Barcelona 5-0.

Laudrup played for Denmark at Euro '84 and helped the side to the semi-final, although they lost on penalties to Spain. At Mexico '86, the Danes beat Scotland, and then Laudrup scored a wonderful solo goal to overcome Uruguay 6-1. They also beat West Germany to top their group, but the side was well beaten by Spain in the round of 16. Denmark also performed uncharacteristically poorly at Euro '88 and didn't win a match, and the side then failed to qualify for the 1990 World Cup.

Laudrup played in the qualifying campaign for the 1992 European Championships but he then quit, citing differences with coach Richard Møller Nielsen. Denmark failed to make it to the championships but were handed a lifeline when Yugoslavia were excluded from the tournament due to the civil war. Laudrup didn't rate Denmark's chances so he remained in exile. Denmark then surprised planet football by winning the tournament, beating the Dutch in the semi and West Germany in the final.

Laudrup returned to the fold for the qualifying campaign for the 1994 World

Cup but Spain and the Republic of Ireland beat them to the finals. Euro '96 was another disappointment but one of the most gifted players of his generation went out on a high after leading the national team to the quarter-final of the 1998 World Cup. He provided a stunning assist for Ebbe Sand in their match against Nigeria and Denmark only went out to Brazil 3-2.

Spain's Raúl and Brazil's Romário rated Laudrup the best they ever played with and the fifth best footballer of all time. If he'd been a little more selfish he would have undoubtedly scored more goals, and some believed he was so good he didn't need to give 100% to be the best player on the pitch. He has been equally laconic but still successful as a manager having been in charge at Brondby, Getafe, Spartak Moscow, RCD Mallorca and latterly Swansea in the Premier League where he won the Capital One (League) Cup during his first season in charge in 2013.

---

**Name:** Michael Laudrup
**Born:** June 15th 1964, Frederiksberg, Denmark
**Position:** Attacking midfielder
**International Career:** 1982 - 1998
**Caps:** 104
**Goals:** 37
**Honours:** Confederations Cup Winner (1995), FIFA World Cup All-Star Team (1998)

# Liedholm

Nils Leidholm played for the youth team in the town of his birth. In 1943 He joined IK Sleipner and earned a reputation as an attacking midfielder with an eye for goal (24 in 60 league starts). He continued in this rich vein of form with IFK Norrköping (22 in 48 league games between 1946 and 1949) and was selected for the national team at the 1948 Olympics. Sweden beat Austria (3-0) and then thrashed South Korea (12-0) with Liedholm scoring twice. They then hammered Denmark in the semi-final and beat Yugoslavia 3-1 in the final.

His performances attracted the attention of AC Milan and he transferred to the Italian side in 1949. Over the next 12 years he racked up four league titles and 89 goals in 394 starts. He captained the side against the all-conquering Real Madrid team in the final of the 1958 European Cup, but Milan lost 3-2 after extra time. Two stories about the great man are shrouded in mystery but both can be believed: it is said that he refused to swap shirts with Alfredo di Stéfano after the match because people would only remember the result; the second story posits that he didn't misplace a pass at the San Siro for the first two years of his spell in Italy. When he finally played a poor pass, the home fans gave him a standing ovation.

Liedholm captained the national team at the 1958 World Cup on home soil and led them to victories over Mexico and Hungary in the group phase, and then the Soviet Union and West Germany in the knockout stage. Liedholm opened the scoring in the final against Brazil but the South Americans had a little-known 17-year-old in their side who would go on to great things. Pelé scored twice and Sweden were eventually beaten 5-2.

Liedholm retired shortly afterwards but then enjoyed a successful managerial career in Italy. He finally quit the game in 1997 and died ten years later.

**Name:** Nils Liedholm
**Born:** October 8th 1922, Valdemarsvik, Sweden
**Died:** November 5th 2007, Cuccaro Monferrato, Italy
**Position:** Attacking midfielder
**International Career:** 1947 - 1958
**Caps:** 23
**Goals:** 12
**Honours:** Olympic Gold Medal (1948), World Cup Runner-up (1958)

# Lineker

Gary Lineker went to the City of Leicester Boys' Grammar School because they had a strong football team and he didn't fancy playing rugby. He was also a prodigiously talented cricketer and captained the county's school team. He joined Leicester's youth football team in 1976 and graduated to the senior side two years later. His goals helped the team to promotion to the old first division twice in the early 1980s.

Lineker then signed for Everton, and his 40 goals in 57 appearances helped them to second in the league and the FA Cup final, although they lost out to Liverpool in both competitions. His prolific form saw him selected for the national team in 1984, and he played all five games of England's World Cup campaign at Mexico '86.

England started the tournament poorly with a loss to Portugal, and they could then only manage a goal-less draw with Morocco. In the decisive third match, Lineker became only the second Englishman to score a World Cup hat-trick as the side saw off Poland 3-0 and qualified for the second phase. He then scored a brace against Paraguay to set up a mouth-watering clash against Argentina. The two countries had recently been at war over the Falkland Islands so there was a bitter subtext to the match.

Maradona scored one of the most controversial goals in the tournament's history when he punched the ball into England's net, but his second was unforgettable for the right reasons. He ran the tiring English defence ragged and slid the ball past Peter Shilton. Lineker scored a consolation goal late on but England were out. His six goals saw him win the Golden Boot and he was also named in the team of the tournament.

Lineker was suffering with hepatitis during England's dismal showing at Euro '88 but he was back to his best at Italia '90. England were again lacklustre in their opening two matches but they then beat Egypt to progress to the knockout phase. They won a tough

England nearly snatched the match in the dying seconds but Chris Waddle's shot hit the inside of the post and rebounded away from goal. The Germans then won the shootout.

Lineker retired after being substituted by Graham Taylor against Sweden at Euro '92. He was one goal short of Bobby Charlton's England record. He continued to enjoy domestic success with Barcelona and Tottenham, and eventually finished with 330 goals from 647 starts. He was never booked in his career and went on to enjoy a second career as a broadcaster and presenter.

game against Belgium and then one of the best games of the tournament against Cameroon. Lineker scored two penalties to overcome a brave African challenge and set up an epic semi-final against Germany.

Andreas Brehme put the Germans ahead after the ball cannoned off Paul Parker and looped over Shilton but Lineker equalised with ten minutes left.

**Name:** Gary Winston Lineker OBE
**Born:** November 30th 1960, Leicester, England
**Position:** Striker
**International Career:** 1984 – 1992
**Caps:** 80
**Goals:** 48
**Honours:** World Cup Golden Boot (1986), World Cup All-Star Team (1986), World Cup Fourth Place (1990)

# Maier

Maier was another one-club man who spent his entire career with Bayern Munich. He joined the youth side aged 14 and made his debut for the senior team four years later, for whom he would play another 535 matches over the next 17 years. Of these, 442 were consecutive appearances in the Bundesliga, which is still a national record.

Maier played 15 times for the German youth and amateur sides in the early 1960s and his solid form saw him selected as understudy to Hans Tilkowski at the 1966 World Cup in England. Four years later in Mexico, Maier helped Germany to the semifinal, but he couldn't prevent Italy winning an epic match 4–3 after extra time.

He was at the peak of his ability for the World Cup on home soil in 1974, however, and he was blessed to be playing alongside such legendary players as Franz Beckenbauer, Berti Vogts, Paul Breitner and Gerd Müller. The mercurial Johan Cruyff ghosted into the penalty area in the opening seconds of the final and was brought down by Uli Hoeness. Johan Neeskens converted the spot-kick but the Germans didn't let the disappointment

get to them. They rallied and were also awarded a penalty, which Breitner scored. Müller scored the winner shortly before half time but Maier was still on hand to deny the Dutch an equalizer and Germany lifted the trophy in his hometown.

Having led the side to the European Championship in 1972, he took Germany to the final of the same tournament four years later, but Antonin Panenka's delicate chipped penalty was too good and Germany were beaten by Czechoslovakia. Maier graced the world stage once more, at the 1978 World Cup in Argentina, although by then he was past his best. Germany failed to get past the second round and the great keeper retired the following year.

He mentored Oliver Kahn, was national goalkeeping coach for 16 years (1988 - 2004) and fulfilled the same role with Bayern Munich until 2008.

**Above:** *Sepp Maier holds the FIFA World Cup aloft in 1974*

**Name:** Josef Dieter 'Sepp' Maier
**Born:** February 28th 1944, Metten, Germany
**Position:** Goalkeeper
**International Career:** 1966 - 1979
**Caps:** 95
**Goals:** 0
**Honours:** European Championship Winner (1972), World Cup Winner (1974)

# Maldini

Although ill fortune denied him the highest international honours, at domestic level Paolo Maldini remains one of the greatest footballers of all time. In 1985 he made his league debut for AC Milan aged only 16. It was the first game of a career that would span nearly a quarter of a century with the same club. When he retired in 2009, he'd amassed 1,028 senior games, of which an incredible 647 were in the league. He also appeared in a record eight Champions League finals, winning five.

Maldini's father Cesare was coach of the national under-21 side and the youngster graduated to the senior squad for a match against Yugoslavia in 1988. He immediately cemented his place and played in every game at Euro '88 and in the World Cup on home soil two years later. Although Italy lost to Argentina on penalties in the semi-final, Maldini put the disappointment behind him and captained the side for much of the next World Cup in the USA. Italy reached the final but were again beaten on penalties, this time by Brazil. He was named in the team

of the tournament 32 years after his father received the same honour.

Italy were poor at Euro '96 and France '98 but they then reached the final of Euro 2000, although Maldini suffered yet another heartbreaking defeat, this time to the French. Italy were eliminated in the round of 16 at the 2002 World Cup so Maldini retired from the international scene without a major trophy, scant reward for a man with superb technique and ability, one of the best readers of the game yet, and a player who led his country a record 74 times. Milan retired the number three jersey in his honour, although Maldini may ask for one of his sons to inherit it as they both play for the youth side.

**Name:** Paolo Cesare Maldini
**Born:** June 26th 1968, Milan, Italy
**Position:** Defender
**International Career:** 1988 - 2002
**Caps:** 126
**Goals:** 7
**Honours:** World Cup Runner-up (1994), European Championship Runner-up (2000)

# Maradona

No player in the history of football has divided opinion as much as Diego Maradona. He could be brilliant, brutal, sublime and ridiculous in a single match, so his 22-year playing career was littered with controversial moments that have come to define him as a man.

He was raised in a shantytown on the outskirts of Buenos Aires and played street football every waking moment. He was soon spotted playing for Estrella Roja and asked to entertain the crowds with his skills during half-time of Argentinos Juniors games. He soon graduated from ball boy to the senior team and made his debut a few days shy of his 16th birthday. He was a sensation, scoring 115 goals in 167 appearances before signing for Boca Juniors in 1981. The following year he came to the attention of Barcelona and joined them for a world-record fee (£5 million). Although he scored 38 goals in 58 games, his time in Spain was marred by injury (opposition defenders deliberately tried to take him out of the game), a bout of hepatitis, and frequent arguments with

the club's board.

He transferred to Napoli and helped the underperforming Italians to two league titles and three cups. But the player himself was beginning to unravel under the pressure. Every move he made off the pitch was scrutinised by the media and Maradona turned to cocaine, for which he was banned for 15 months in 1991. His domestic career then wound down and ended with two seasons back with Boca Juniors.

His international career was a rollercoaster of supreme highs (a World Cup win as captain), devastating lows (another failed drug test), goals of the highest quality such as that against England in the quarter-final of the 1986 World Cup, and, in the same match, the infamous 'hand of god' goal where he punched the ball into England's net and got away with it.

He made his international debut aged just 16 in 1977 but he was considered too young and inexperienced to be included in the 1978 World Cup squad. Maradona was

## MARADONA

almost inconsolable when his team won the trophy as he felt he should have been playing. The 1982 World Cup in Spain brought him mixed fortunes: he scored twice against Hungary to help his team to the second phase but he was then man-marked by Italy's Claudio Gentile in the first game and sent off for serious foul play in a second loss to Brazil. Indeed Maradona showed the world a violent streak several times throughout his career, and there can be no excuse for his terrible lunge at Atlético Bilbao's Andoni Zubizarreta that left the keeper unconscious. It was a deliberate and shameful knee to the head that could have left Zubizarreta seriously injured (Maradona had already head-butted Sola and elbowed another Bilbao defender in the face).

Maradona was named captain for the 1986 World Cup and he was on sparkling form, providing three assists in the opening game against South Korea, goals against Italy, two against England (the first with the hand, the second pure genius when he left five defenders in his wake and then beat Shilton), two more against Belgium in the semi-final, and the crucial assist for Jorge Burruchaga against West Germany in the final. There is no question that he dragged an ordinary team to the final and then provided the brilliance to win the competition.

Despite playing with an injured ankle, he did the same four years later in Italy, only this time Argentina lost a dour final to a well-organised West German team. Maradona was sent home in disgrace from USA '94 after failing a second drug test. More controversy followed when he shot several reporters with an air rifle because he felt they were invading his privacy.

In 2000 he was admitted to hospital having taken cocaine – he was apparently addicted for much of his later career – and damage to the heart was diagnosed. Four years later he suffered a drug-induced heart attack and was lucky to survive.

He underwent gastric bypass surgery and attended rehab but he was readmitted to hospital in 2007 and treated for hepatitis and alcohol abuse.

Maradona somehow found the will to turn his life round and only a year later, with hardly any top-flight coaching experience, he was named as manager of Argentina. The side topped their group at the 2010 World Cup in South Africa but eventually lost to Germany in the quarter-final and his contract wasn't renewed.

Maradona's ability is unquestioned: he was short and compact and this low centre of gravity allowed him to change direction and beat opposing defenders with searing pace or devastating skill. His left foot was much stronger but he also played in team-mates with deft touches from his right. He was named joint (with Pelé) best player of the 20th century and remains an iconic figure, a living god to his legions of fans.

**Name:** Diego Armando Maradona (Franco)
**Born:** October 30th 1960, Buenos Aires, Argentina
**Position:** Attacking midfielder / striker
**International Career:** 1977 - 1994
**Caps:** 91
**Goals:** 34
**Honours:** World Cup Winner (1986), World Cup Runner-up (1990)

# Masopust

**Right:** *Josef Masopust playing for Dukla Prague*

Josef Masopust spent two years with ZSJ Technomat Teplice before signing for Dukla Prague in 1952. His tireless running in the midfield broke up opponents' attacks before his pinpoint passing and deft on-the-ball skills enabled his team to counter. He could use both feet equally and often went on mazy dribbles that left defenders utterly confused. He may have been slightly built but he was rarely dispossessed because he had such pace and awareness. Over the next 16 years he scored 79 league goals in 386 appearances, but it is for the national team that he made the biggest impression.

He first played for Czechoslovakia in 1954 but he wasn't selected for the World Cup squad. His first international goal came against Switzerland in a 6-1 victory and he was in great form before the 1958 World Cup in Sweden. Despite the Czechs thrashing Argentina 6-1 and drawing 2-2 with West Germany, a shock loss to Northern Ireland in their opening match meant they had to play the Irish again in a playoff, which they also lost.

Masopust put the hugely disappointing campaign behind him and was in his prime for the 1962 World Cup in Chile. The Czechs beat Spain and drew with Brazil to squeeze through from a difficult group, and they then beat Hungary and Yugoslavia to reach the final against Brazil. Masopust opened the scoring but goals from Amarildo, Zito and Vavá saw Brazil retain the trophy. Czechoslovakia didn't qualify for the 1966 World Cup so Masopust retired with 10 goals from his 63 caps. He moved into management in 1973 with his former club and took charge of the national team from 1984 until 1987.

**Name:** Josef Masopust
**Born:** February 9th 1931, Strimice, Czechoslovakia
**Position:** Midfielder
**International Career:** 1954 – 1966
**Caps:** 63
**Goals:** 10
**Honours:** World Cup Runner-up (1962)

# Matthäus

Lothar Matthäus started his career with local side FC Herzogenaurach in Bavaria but he joined top-flight outfit Borussia Mönchengladbach at the age of 18. He made such an impact on the Bundesliga that he was selected for the national team at Euro '80 the following year. West Germany won the tournament and they were fancied to do well at the 1982 World Cup in Spain. Despite losing their opening match to Algeria, they bounced back with comfortable wins over Chile and Austria. They then overcame the hosts in the second phase to set up a semi-final against France. West Germany edged past the French in a brilliant but brutal match, but they weren't strong enough to overcome a Paolo Rossi-inspired Italy in the final.

He had to endure the heartbreak of a World Cup final defeat again four years later in Mexico. Assigned to mark Diego Maradona, Matthäus allowed the mercurial Argentine only a couple of moments of space in the entire match, but it was enough for Maradona to supply the killer pass that gave them a 3-2 victory. Maradona later said that Matthäus was the best rival he'd ever had, but that was scant consolation.

The two came up against one another at the third consecutive World Cup when the sides faced off in the final of Italia '90. It had been a dour tournament of largely defensive tactics but Matthäus's West Germany were one of the few sides to employ an attacking formation. This time Matthäus got the recognition his talent deserved and West Germany won a poor match 1-0. As captain of the side, Matthäus had the honour of lifting the FIFA World Cup.

He continued to win domestic silverware with Bayern Munich and Internazionale, and he was selected as a sweeper for USA '94, his fourth World Cup. The Germans were dumped out in the quarter-final by an un-fancied Bulgaria and Matthäus was then left out of the side for Euro '96, a tournament which Germany won. In being recalled for the 1998 World Cup in France, Matthäus became only the second player (and the first outfield player) after Mexican goalkeeper Antonio Carbajal

**Above:** *Lothar Matthäus scores a penalty against Bulgaria at the 1994 World Cup in the USA*

to appear in five World Cups. He extended his own record when playing his 25th World Cup match, a defeat to Croatia in the quarter-final.

He earned three more caps for Germany at Euro 2000 but the side was eliminated at the group stage. A move into coaching was less distinguished but Matthäus remains one of the greatest midfielders the game has produced.

**Name:** Lothar Herbert Matthäus
**Born:** March 21st 1961, Erlangen, Germany
**Position:** Sweeper / midfielder
**International Career:** 1980 - 2000
**Caps:** 150
**Goals:** 23
**Honours:** European Championship Winner (1980), World Cup Runner-up (1982, 1986), World Cup Winner (1990)

# Miller

Roger Milla or Miller was born in the Cameroonian capital but he didn't settle for playing with a single youth side as his father's job on the railways meant the family was always on the move. In 1971 he signed for Léopard and immediately made a name for himself as a finisher of considerable talent (89 league goals in 117 games). His prolific goal-scoring continued with various clubs – including Tonnerre in his homeland, and Monaco, Saint-Étienne and Montpelier in France – which led to a call up to the national team.

Cameroon went out at the group phase in 1982 after drawing all their matches and Milla seemed destined to fade into obscurity when he announced his retirement in 1987. Three years later, however, Cameroonian President Paul Biya begged him to reconsider and join the Indomitable Lions at Italia '90. Milla was 38 and out of shape but he agreed and became an overnight sensation. He scored twice against Romania and twice more against Colombia to secure a quarter-final berth.

He then came off the bench against England, won a penalty and set up Ekeke with a delightful touch to give Cameroon the lead. England fought back to win 3-2 after extra time but Milla – with his trademark dance around the corner flag after every goal – was the star of the tournament. He reprised the super-sub role in the USA four years later and, at the age of 42, he became the oldest scorer in World Cup history when he notched against Russia.

**Above:** *Roger Miller steals the ball from Colombian goalkeeper René Higuita at Italia '90*

| | |
|---|---|
| **Name:** | (Albert) Roger (Mooh) Miller |
| **Born:** | May 20th 1952, Yaoundé, Cameroon |
| **Position:** | Striker |
| **International Career:** | 1973 - 1994 |
| **Caps:** | 102 |
| **Goals:** | 28 |
| **Honours:** | African Player of the Century |

# Moore

Bobby Moore played football for his school before being signed by West Ham in 1956. He had to wait two years for his debut against Manchester United because Malcolm Allison had been in his position. Allison was suffering from tuberculosis, however, so Moore stepped in and made the central defensive position his own. He quickly developed into an unflappable presence at the back with great technique and the ability to read the game like no other.

He progressed so rapidly with his club that he was called up to the national side as cover during the 1962 World Cup in Chile. He made his debut in a 4-0 pre-tournament win over Peru and was so impressive that he started every game at the finals. England lost to eventual winners Brazil in the quarter-final but the legend had already been born. Moore went on to captain England the following year at just 22, and Alf Ramsey gave him the armband on a permanent basis in 1964.

England progressed easily from their group at the 1966 World Cup, and they managed to overcome an overtly aggressive Argentina in the quarter-final and a Eusébio-inspired Portugal in the semi to set up a mouthwatering final against Franz Beckenbauer's West Germany. Alf Ramsey was concerned about Moore's lack of pace and considered dropping the skipper for the final but good sense prevailed and Moore led England onto the Wembley turf.

Although they went behind to a Helmut Haller strike, Moore took a quick free-kick for Geoff Hurst to head home the equalizer. Both sides scored again and the match went to extra time. Hurst scored his hotly debated second before Moore picked him out with a beautiful long ball to complete his hat-trick in the dying seconds. Moore became a hero and national icon overnight.

The side reached the semi-final of the 1968 European Championships before flying out to Mexico to defend the World Cup in 1970. England's preparations were disrupted when Moore was accused and later exonerated for allegedly stealing

a bracelet but it didn't detract from his superb on-field performances, particularly in a memorable game against eventual champions Brazil when he timed several important tackles to perfection. The tournament ended in disappointment, however, when West Germany avenged their defeat in the final four years earlier by overcoming a two-goal deficit to win their quarter-final in extra time.

His career gradually declined thereafter, and he was blamed by many for giving the ball away in a crucial qualifier for the 1974 World Cup that saw Poland go to the finals at England's expense. It was a slightly sad end to a magnificent international career that had seen him lift the Jules Rimet Trophy and equal Billy Wright's record of 90 appearances as captain. But the final word on Moore – who died of cancer in 1993 – should go to his most illustrious opponent, Pelé: "He was the greatest defender I ever played against." There's no higher praise than that.

**Name:** Robert Frederick Chelsea 'Bobby' Moore OBE
**Born:** April 12th 1941, Barking, England
**Died:** February 24th 1993, Wandsworth
**Position:** Defender
**International Career:** 1962 - 1973
**Caps:** 108
**Goals:** 2
**Honours:** World Cup Winner (1966)

# Müller

S hort but powerfully built, Gerd Müller had a predatory instinct in front of goal and he developed into a scoring machine for club and country. An oft-repeated quote sums up his outstanding ability to score from the most unlikely situations: "He can score standing up, lying down, sitting down and even when falling over. He scores with his head, with his right and left foot, with the knee, his heel and with his toes. Müller even strikes with his stomach and backside."

Gerhard Müller was born in Bavaria in November 1945 and he began playing football with local side TSV 1861 Nördlingen in 1963. He started as he meant to continue, scoring 46 goals in only 31 games, and Bayern Munich soon snapped him up. Although they were in a lower league, Müller's goals helped them to promotion. The following season they finished third in the top flight, won the German Cup and qualified for the European Cup Winners' Cup. They then won the Bundesliga and German Cup double in the 1968 season, with Müller contributing 31 goals in 30 games.

Bayern won the league and cup double again in 1972, 1973 and 1974 and they also began to dominate in Europe, winning the European Champions Cup in 1974, 1975 and 1976, a year in which they also won the Intercontinental Cup. His domestic tally of 365 goals in 427 league appearances, 80 goals in 64 German Cup games, and 66 goals in 74 European appearances are records that are likely to stand for some time.

He made his international debut against Turkey in 1966 and mirrored his domestic success in the West German team. Der Bomber eventually scored 68 goals in 62 internationals, his peak coinciding with the 1970 World Cup in Mexico. He scored the winner against Morocco, hat-tricks against Bulgaria and Peru, an extra-time winner against England in the quarter-final, and two goals in the semi-final against Italy, although in the latter his heroics were in a losing cause.

His goals finally brought the national team some silverware at the 1972

European Championships in Belgium. Müller scored twice in the semi-final and the final as Germany defeated Belgium and Russia respectively. He retired from international football after sealing victory against the Dutch in the 1974 World Cup final. Müller's record of 14 World Cup goals was only beaten by Ronaldo in 2006, although the Brazilian needed four tournaments to score 15 goals while Müller only played in two.

As with so many other stars of the 1970s, Müller moved to America for a couple of seasons and added 40 more goals in 80 matches. Life after such a glittering career in football was not easy but he recovered from alcoholism to become youth and amateur coach at Bayern Munich. In 2006 he was Munich's ambassador during the World Cup on home soil.

**Name:** Gerhard 'Gerd' Müller
**Born:** November 3rd 1945, Nördlingen, Germany
**Position:** Striker
**International Career:** 1966 - 1974
**Caps:** 62
**Goals:** 68
**Honours:** European Championship Winner (1972), World Cup Winner (1974)

# Neeskens

Johan Neeskens began playing for his local side, RCH Heemstede, in 1968. Two years later he'd signed for Ajax having been spotted by Rinus Michels, and he then became an integral part of the total-football system employed by the Dutch in the 1970s. Ajax won three consecutive European Cups in that period and Neeskens – who'd now moved from right-back to midfield – provided the perfect foil for Johan Cruyff with his limitless stamina, superb technique and powerful shot.

Neeskens was called up to the national squad in 1970 for a match against East Germany, but it wasn't until four years later at the World Cup in Germany that he showcased his talents to the wider world. The Dutch beat Uruguay and Bulgaria in the first group stage before embarrassing Argentina (4-0), East Germany (2-0) and Brazil (also 2-0) in the second round. They'd only conceded one goal en route to the final, and that was a Krol own goal.

Neeskens scored from the spot in the final against West Germany before the hosts had even touched the ball, but then Dutch swagger was gradually eroded by the tireless German effort. The hosts eventually scored twice, consigning Dutch mastery to defeat by German efficiency. It was a bitter blow for the fans of total football but the Dutch were back to their best four years later in Argentina.

Despite being injured in the loss to Scotland, Neeskens was instrumental in his side's march to their second successive final. The hosts were again too strong, however, with Argentina scoring twice in injury time to the lift the World Cup. He retired in 1981 with 49 caps under his belt. A decade later Neeskens moved into management but he didn't enjoy the same success and hasn't worked in football since 2012.

**Name:** Johannnes Jacobus 'Johan' Neeskens
**Born:** September 15th 1951, Heemstede, Netherlands
**Position:** Midfield
**International Career:** 1970 - 1981
**Caps:** 49
**Goals:** 17
**Honours:** World Cup Runner-up (1974, 1978)

# Overath

Wolfgang Overath enjoyed a nine-year youth career with SSV Siegburg before he joined FC Köln in 1962. In the next 15 years he cemented his reputation as one of the most gifted playmakers of his generation. He was selected for the national side in 1963, and, alongside Franz Beckenbauer, he guided West Germany to the World Cup final three years later.

Despite having a good game, Overath couldn't prevent hosts England winning an epic match 4-2 after extra time. Four years later he was still the outstanding midfield general in the West German side and he helped avenge the defeat to England in the quarter-final of Mexico '70. Trailing 2-0, Beckenbauer and Overath suddenly found themselves with the freedom of the park when Ramsey substituted Bobby Charlton. The English couldn't deal with the marauding maestros and Müller smashed home a close-range winner in extra time. West Germany came up short against Italy in an epic semi-final but they then won the playoff to claim third place.

Overath finally earned a winner's medal at the 1974 World Cup on home soil, thereby becoming only one of two players (the other being team-mate Beckenbauer) to have medals for coming third, second and first at the tournament. He probably should have made more appearances for his country but he had to fight for his place with the equally prodigious Günter Netzer during the same period. Not many midfielders can claim 287 goals in 765 domestic appearances, and he remains one of the finest German players of all time.

**Above:** *Wolfgang Overath and Gerd Müller celebrate after winning the 1974 World Cup final against the Dutch*

**Name:** Wolfgang Overath
**Born:** September 29th 1943, Siegburg, Germany
**Position:** Midfielder
**International Career:** 1963 – 1974
**Caps:** 81
**Goals:** 17
**Honours:** World Cup Runner-up (1966), World Cup Winner 1974

# Passarella

Daniel Passarella started his career with Sarmiento in 1971 and he immediately forged a reputation as a goal-scoring sweeper. He then signed for River Plate and netted a barely believable 90 goals in just 226 appearances, unthinkable for a central defender. He couldn't ignore the attention from the giants of European football so he moved to Fiorentina for five seasons in the 1980s before a brief spell with Internazionale in Milan. He played out the remainder of his domestic career with River Plate.

Such was his influence at club level that he was first selected for his country in 1974, but it wasn't until the World Cup on home soil in 1978 that he became a household name as captain of Argentina. He led the side by example and with great skill and bravery as they notched up wins against Hungary and France. Defeat to Italy in the final group match was inconsequential as they still qualified for the second phase.

There was plenty of controversy in the second round because previous results meant that Argentina needed to beat Peru by four goals to reach the final at the expense of archrivals Brazil. However unlikely this seemed – Peru were a decent side that had drawn with the magnificent Dutch and beaten Scotland and Iran in the first round – they inexplicably capitulated in the second half against the hosts and Argentina won 6-0. Whether victory was achieved by fair means or foul has been debated ever since and it remains an unproven case. Argentina won the final against the Dutch and Passarella became the first man from his country to lift the FIFA World Cup. He was sidelined for the 1986 tournament in Mexico although, as part of the squad, he did receive a winner's medal after the final against West Germany.

Although he was diminutive in height and build, he was deceptively quick and powerful, and he often finished off moves begun inside his own half with searing forward runs and a devastating shot. His

tally of 140 goals in 451 league appearances was a record for a defender until it was beaten by free-kick specialist Ronald Koeman. He proved to be a controversial coach when he banned long hair, earrings and homosexuals from Argentina's 1998 squad in France and several of the team refused to play for him.

**Name:** Daniel Alberto Passarella
**Born:** May 25th 1953, Chacabuco, Argentina
**Position:** Central defender
**International Career:** 1974 - 1986
**Caps:** 70
**Goals:** 22
**Honours:** World Cup Winner (1978, 1986)

**Above:** *Daniel Passarella with the World Cup in 1978*

# Pelé

Pelé is the embodiment of Brazilian football, playing the game to a samba beat with spellbinding flair and creativity. His autobiography coined the phrase 'The Beautiful Game' and there can be no more fitting description of his style of play and ability. Pelé played as an inside forward, striker and playmaker with visionary passing, slalom-like dribbling, and an almost supernatural goal-scoring ability. He holds the record for being the youngest winner of the World Cup and is the only player to have won the title three times. After collecting his third winner's medal, the headline in the English newspaper, *The Times*, read: "How do you spell Pelé? G-O-D."

Pelé was born in Minais Gerais, a state in the southeast of Brazil. He had a fairly typical Brazilian upbringing, living in a small and crowded house with a leaking roof. His family struggled to make ends meet but he ended up playing football in the streets with his friends. Unable to afford a real football, they would play with a sock stuffed with newspapers and rags and tied up with string. Despite material hardship, it was a close family and his parents taught him to respect the innate qualities of people, the importance of keeping a promise, and to live with dignity. It was these personal qualities that people around the world would come to love, as much as the sublime football he played.

He was still a child when the family moved to Baurú in the interior of São Paolo state. His father, Dondinho, was also a professional player but a serious knee injury ended his career prematurely. Dondinho became the young Edson's first coach and biggest fan but his dad originally nicknamed him Dico (he ended up fighting with schoolmates who called him Pelé). Having stood by his father, his mother worried about the insecurity of a footballer's life and wanted something better for her son. Pelé wanted to help supplement his family's income so he began shining shoes but he made little money and convinced his mother to allow him to work at the Baurú Athletic Club stadium on match days and at the railway

stations in town. It was around this time that his aunt Maria gave him his first pair of shoes, which had belonged to her boss's son. He was only allowed to wear them for church and special occasions but he soon ruined them playing football.

Aged 11 he was playing for an amateur team called Ameriquinha when he was spotted by former World Cup star Waldemar de Brito. De Brito asked him to join the youth team he coached and, when he reached 15, Waldemar took him for a trial at Santos football club in São Paolo. Waldemar declared to a disbelieving board that Pelé would become the greatest soccer player in the world. Pelé soon made his senior team debut, scoring as a substitute in September 1956 when he was still only 15. In the first league game he played for Santos he scored four goals. The next season he established himself in the first team and finished as São Paolo state's top scorer with 32 goals.

Pelé's meteoric rise continued and he made his international debut against Argentina in 1957, scoring the only goal

in a 2-1 loss. However, at the 1958 World Cup in Sweden, the virtually unknown 17-year-old thrilled the world and became an instant legend. After Brazil's two opening group games, Pelé made his World Cup entrance against the USSR. Although he did not score, Brazil won 2-0. In the quarter-final Pelé scored the only goal to knock Wales out, before scoring a hat-trick in a 5-2 demolition of France to put Brazil into the final. The final was a classic encounter littered with attacking football and flair and Brazil hammered hosts Sweden 5-2 to win the World Cup for the first time. Pelé scored twice: the first saw him control the ball on his chest, flick a beautiful but precise lob over the

**Above:** *Pelé in training for Brazil's match against England*

Pelé was a global sensation. Brazil started with a 2-0 victory over Mexico, Pelé scoring a wonder goal after dribbling past four players and then beating the 'keeper. However, ten minutes into the next match against Czechoslovakia he pulled a thigh muscle trying a long-range shot and did not play again. Brazil won the trophy by beating Czechoslovakia 3-1 when they faced each other again in the final.

With the elite European clubs trying to sign him, it is rumoured that the government of Brazil declared Pelé an official national treasure to prevent him moving overseas. If 1962 had been a disappointment, 1966 was even worse as Brazil struggled in England. They lost against Hungary 3-1 (during which Pelé was rested), before playing against a violent Portuguese side. They literally kicked him out of the tournament in the first group stage, much to the disgust of spectators and commentators. Pelé announced that he would not play in another World Cup after such treatment and a lack of protection from the referees.

In 1967, his appearance with Santos during a short tour of exhibition matches in Nigeria resulted in a 48-hour ceasefire in the Biafran Civil War so that both sides could watch him play. Pelé hit another

nearest defender, before nipping round to volley into the net. Pelé, the youngest winner of the World Cup, crying tears of joy while being hugged by his team-mates after the final whistle, remains an iconic image from the tournament.

Pelé continued his phenomenal form with Santos, where he was top scorer every season from 1957 to 1965, during which Santos dominated the Campeonato Paulista (state league championship). Santos soon capitalised on the Black Pearl's fame and travelled the world to play exhibition matches against its top teams (Pelé received a percentage from each game and became one of the era's best-paid athletes).

By the 1962 World Cup finals in Chile,

incredible milestone by scoring his 1,000th goal, a penalty, against Vasco da Gama in 1969. Known as O Milésimo (The Thousandth), it was widely celebrated in Brazil, and he dedicated it to all the poor children in the country.

Luckily for Brazil and planet football, Pelé was persuaded to return for his fourth World Cup in Mexico in 1970. Playing alongside Jairzinho, Rivelino, Carlos Alberto, Gérson, and Tostão, he was sensational, and many believe they formed the nucleus of the best team ever assembled. They were drawn in a tough group that included Czechoslovakia, Romania and defending world champions England. Brazil beat Czechoslovakia 4-1, with Pelé scoring one and narrowly missing an audacious chip over Czech goalkeeper Ivo Viktor from the halfway line. In an unforgettable and high-quality match, England defended brilliantly but were eventually beaten 1-0 by a Jairzinho goal (set up by Pelé).

Pelé had seemed certain to score with a bullet header earlier in the match but Gordon Banks somehow denied him with a flying dive to scoop the ball away before it crossed the line. It is commonly referred to as the 'Save of the Century' and Pelé called it the best save he had ever seen.

He opened the scoring against Romania from a free-kick and then added a second to secure a 3-2 win. In the quarter-final Brazil beat Peru 4-2, before they defeated Uruguay 3-1 in the semi-final. The game also contained another piece of Pelé brilliance as he broke free of the defence to chase a ball knocked into space by Tostão. Uruguayan keeper Ladislao Mazurkiewicz raced off his line to meet the ball, but Pelé dummied and let the ball right as he ran left, leaving the keeper in no-man's land. Pelé then turned and shot but he dragged the ball narrowly wide. Brazil outplayed Italy in the final, running out 4-1 winners. Pelé scored a header and claimed two assists and Brazil were crowned champions for an unprecedented third time. They were allowed to keep the Jules Rimet trophy permanently.

Pelé wanted to retire while still at the top so he played his last international in a 2-2 draw against Yugoslavia in 1971. He stayed with Santos for four more successful years, eventually retiring in 1974, after which Santos retired his number ten jersey in tribute. However, he was soon tempted out of retirement to play in the lucrative North American Soccer League (NASL) for the New York Cosmos in a multi-million-dollar deal (rumoured to be worth between

**Above:** *Pelé celebrates his headed goal against Italy in the 1970 World Cup final*

$2.8 million and $4.5 million). Despite being past his prime, he still sparkled and brought a level of glamour to the NASL before he retired for good in 1977. His last game was an emotional exhibition match against Santos. He played one half for each team before being carried on his colleagues' shoulders around the Giants' stadium in front of a capacity crowd.

After such an illustrious career, Pelé devoted much of his time to charities helping underprivileged children through the United Nations Children Fund (UNICEF), as well as being made Brazil's Minister of Sport for three years. As well as advertising sponsorship, he has written an autobiography, and appeared in a number of films and documentaries, including starring alongside Michael Caine and Sylvester Stallone in the 1981 classic *Escape to Victory*. He is still an influential presence on football's global stage and is revered around the world for his skill, his passion for the beautiful game, his sportsmanship and his humility.

**Name:** Pelé (Edson Arantes do Nascimento)
**Born:** October 23rd 1940, Três Corações, Brazil
**Position:** Striker
**International Career:** 1957 – 1971
**Caps:** 92
**Goals:** 77
**Honours:** World Cup Winner (1958, 1962, 1970)

# Platini

A gifted attacking midfield playmaker with superb technical ability, Frenchman Michel Platini was so comfortable on the ball that he was almost invariably the best player on the pitch. He was deadly in front of goal for club and country in the 1980s and now works for UEFA in an official capacity.

Michel François Platini was born in June 1955 in Lorraine, France. Unlike his contemporaries who played professionally having been to the sporting academies, Platini learned to play with friends in the street. His father started coaching him and reminded him that moving the ball quickly with accurate passing rather than running with it and losing control was the way to keep possession.

While playing for youth side AS Jœuf, he attracted interest from FC Metz but he was injured during his trial and then failed a fitness test. Despite a poor prognosis from the club doctor, he joined AS Nancy-Lorraine in 1972. As he was establishing himself in the squad, he broke his arm, was unable to play and Nancy were relegated, but he scored vital goals the following season and they were promoted as champions.

Platini made his international debut against Czechoslovakia in 1976 and was then selected for the French Olympic team. He was also named in the 1978 World Cup squad but France couldn't progress from a tough group. Despite losing to England in the opening game at the 1982 World Cup, the French then beat Kuwait, Austria and Northern Ireland before they eventually lost to the brutal but brilliant Germans in the semi-final.

Platini's best tournament would be the 1984 European Championships on home turf, however. With Alain Giresse, Luis Fernández and Jean Tigana, Platini completed the carré magique (or magic square), the elegant midfield formation at the heart of the team. Platini was unstoppable, scoring nine of his country's 14 goals in their five matches, which included the winner in the semi-final and the opener in the final against Spain.

**Right:** *Michel Platini of France*

On the domestic front, Platini moved to AS Saint-Étienne when his Nancy contract expired in 1979. He enjoyed moderate success for three years before moving to Juventus where he won numerous honours: the Italian Cup in 1983, the Scudetto in 1984 and 1986, the European Cup Winners' Cup and Super Cup in 1984, the European Champions Cup and Intercontinental Cup in 1985, and the European Footballer of the Year trophy three times, in 1983, 1984, and 1985 (when he was top scorer in the Italian league).

Platini was carrying a groin injury and needed injections to play at the World Cup in Mexico (1986) but he scored vital goals against Italy and Brazil, although the French lost again to West Germany in the semi-final. It was no coincidence that Platini's international retirement brought about a decline in fortunes for the French national team and they failed to qualify for Euro '88 or the 1990 World Cup.

As coach of the national team, he couldn't replicate his former success and he resigned after a poor showing at Euro '92 in Sweden. Today, he is President of UEFA, a position he has held since 2006.

**Name:** Michel François Platini
**Born:** June 21st 1955, Jœuf, France
**Position:** Attacking midfield
**International Career:** 1976 - 1987
**Caps:** 72
**Goals:** 41
**Honours:** European Championship Winner (1984), World Cup Third Place (1986)

# Puskás

Ferenc Puskás began his career with Kispest AC under the tutelage of his father who was their coach. The side was commandeered by the military in 1949 and underwent a name change to Budapest Honvéd. Under army rules, the players were given ranks, which is how Puskás earned the nickname the 'Galloping Major'. The side used its influence to recruit the finest footballers in the country so Puskás was soon playing alongside Kocsis, Hidegkuti and Czibor. This nucleus formed a formidable attacking partnership and became part of the Hungarian national side that terrorised defences across Europe for a decade.

Puskás made his debut for the national team in a 5-2 win over Austria in 1945 but he only came to the attention of the wider world at the Helsinki Olympics in 1952. He then scored four goals in Hungary's two seminal encounters against England before the 1954 World Cup. It was widely believed that England, despite having suffered a shock exit at the 1950 World Cup to the USA, would be the dominant force in European football. The likes of Stanley Matthews and Tom Finney were amongst the best in the world, so it came as something of a hammer blow to the English when the illusion of their superiority was shattered by the Mighty Magyars, first at Wembley (6-3) and then in Budapest (7-1). The balance of power in Europe was shifting towards Hungary, Austria and Germany.

This shift was confirmed when Hungary marched to the final of the World Cup in Switzerland. Puskás scored three goals in the first two games but suffered a hairline fracture of the ankle in the 8-3 demolition of West Germany. He was rested until the final but, as the opponents were again Germany, he was selected for what the pundits predicted would be a comfortable win.

Despite being hampered by the injury, Puskás opened the scoring. Hungary were 2-0 up two minutes later but thereafter the heavy conditions and an extremely fit West German team

**Right:** *Ferenc
Puskás shortly
after his retirement
from the game*

Stéfano developed into one of the deadliest strike partnerships and Puskás eventually took Spanish nationality. He played four games for his adopted country, three of which were at the 1962 World Cup. He failed to make an impression and retired after the tournament.

There can be no doubt that Puskás is one of the game's true legends. He scored more than 600 goals in a 19-year career, of which 84 were for Hungary in just 85 appearances. He captained a golden generation of players in a side that was invincible (bar the World Cup final) for 52 matches over six years, an achievement that is unlikely to be equalled.

conspired to overcome them. Helmut Rahn scored the equaliser after only 18 minutes and he netted again in the dying moments to give the Germans the lead but Puskás still had time to find the net. His late strike was deemed offside, however, and the Germans held on for the unlikeliest of wins.

He retired from football but made a surprise return to the domestic game with Real Madrid in 1958. He and Alfredo di

---

**Name:** Ferenc Puskás
**Born:** April 1st 1927, Budapest, Hungary
**Died:** November 17th 2006, Budapest
**Position:** Inside-left
**International Career:** 1945 - 1956
**Caps:** 85
**Goals:** 84
**Honours:** Olympic Gold Medal (1952),
World Cup Runner-up (1954)

# Rahn

Helmut Rahn had a long and distinguished youth career with SV Altenessen, SC Oelde and Sportfreunde Katernberg before he joined Rot-Weiss Essen in 1951. In eight years with the club he scored 88 league goals from 201 starts and was called up to the West German national team.

The side was demolished 8-3 by Hungary in the group stage of the 1954 World Cup in Switzerland but two wins over Turkey, and then more victories over Yugoslavia and Austria saw the Germans through to the final against the mighty Hungarians.

The game has since become known as the Miracle of Bern because a Hungarian side with the likes of Puskás, Bozsik, Hidegkuti, Czibor and Kocsis had thrashed every team they'd faced (including Brazil and World Cup holders Uruguay), were unbeaten in their previous 32 games stretching back to June 1950 and were expected to annihilate the Germans for the second time in the tournament. But German manager Sepp Herberger hadn't played his full team in the earlier match, and wet and windy conditions favoured the Germans with their new Adidas boots.

When Puskás and Czibor put the Magyars 2-0 up after only eight minutes, the game seemed to be panning out as the pundits predicted. The Germans rallied, however, and Rahn added a second after Max Morlock had pulled one back. The Hungarians upped the pressure in the second half but Toni Turek kept the Germans in the match with a series of fine saves. Six minutes from the end, Rahn scored the winner, although there was still time for controversy as Puskás had a late goal disallowed for offside. There was more controversy after the final whistle as it emerged years later that the German players may have been injected with methamphetamine to help them in the latter stages of a gruelling match.

Rahn remains a national hero in Germany for causing one of the biggest upsets in sporting history. Indeed no side has ever held a higher world ranking than Hungary in 1954, so Rahn's goals made the Miracle of Bern a reality.

**Above:** *Helmut Rahn scored two goals in the 1954 World Cup final against Hungary*

---

**Name:** Helmut Rahn
**Born:** August 16th 1929, Essen, Germany
**Died:** August 14th 2003, Essen
**Position:** Wing / forward
**International Career:** 1951 - 1960
**Caps:** 40
**Goals:** 21
**Honours:** World Cup Winner (1954)

---

# Raúl

**Below:** *Raúl in his last season with Real Madrid*

Raúl began playing for San Cristóbal youth team at the age of 10. He then graduated to Real Madrid's senior team via Atlético and Real's development programmes. Over the next 16 years he shattered records that were once considered unbeatable: he scored the most goals for Real Madrid (323), made the most appearances for the side (741), scored the most goals in the history of the Champions League (71), and made a record number of appearances in the competition (132). It is surprising, therefore, that for someone so prolific at domestic level, he never quite lived up to expectations on the international front.

Despite proving himself at Real, Raúl was left out of the Spain squad for Euro '96 and the side was beaten on penalties by England in the quarter-final. Spain hammered Bulgaria 6–1 in their final group match at France '98 but they'd already lost to Nigeria and drawn with Paraguay so they failed to make the knockout phase. They topped their group at Euro 2000 despite losing their first match, but were then beaten by eventual champions France.

By the 2002 World Cup, Spain had the

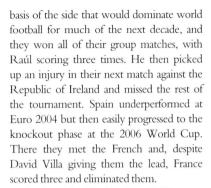

basis of the side that would dominate world football for much of the next decade, and they won all of their group matches, with Raúl scoring three times. He then picked up an injury in their next match against the Republic of Ireland and missed the rest of the tournament. Spain underperformed at Euro 2004 but then easily progressed to the knockout phase at the 2006 World Cup. There they met the French and, despite David Villa giving them the lead, France scored three and eliminated them.

Raúl wasn't picked for Euro 2008 because Fernando Torres and David Villa were the preferred strikers so he retired with a then-record 44 goals from 102 international caps. There's no doubt that Raúl's talent deserved greater reward at international level but poor luck, the odd injury and a side that often choked on the big stage conspired to deny him the trophies his former team-mates are now winning.

---

**Name:** Raúl (González Blanco)
**Born:** June 27th 1977, Madrid, Spain
**Position:** Striker
**International Career:** 1996 – 2006
**Caps:** 102
**Goals:** 44
**Honours:** Champions League Winner (1998, 2000, 2002)

---

# Rensenbrink

Rob Rensenbrink enjoyed a successful youth career with DWS Amsterdam before signing for Door Wilskracht Sterk and then Club Brugge. In 1971 he joined Anderlecht and, over the next nine years, he became a legend in domestic Belgian football and with the Dutch national side. He won two league titles and seven cups with Anderlecht but remained on the fringes of the national team between 1968 and 1974 because there was stiff competition for forward places from the likes of Johan Cruyff and Piet Keizer.

Visionary coach Rinus Michels recognised his talent, and his willingness to adopt the total football style for which the Dutch would become famous, so he was picked for the 1974 World Cup. The Netherlands breezed through their group and then demolished Argentina, East Germany (Rensenbrink sealed victory with a second goal) and Brazil in the second phase. But despite trying to dish out a football master-class to archrivals West Germany in the final,

Franz Beckenbauer's side recovered from an early setback to win the match 2-1. This may have been in part because Rensenbrink played in Belgium so he wasn't as familiar with the rotation system, that Cruyff tended to occupy his usual position, and that he'd picked up a slight injury earlier in the tournament.

He was a mainstay of the side during the qualifying campaign and tournament proper for the 1976 European Championships but the Netherlands were beaten by Czechoslovakia in the semi-final. Rensenbrink was still in the side for the 1978 World Cup, however, and he scored a hat-trick against Iran and another goal in a shock loss to Scotland. Despite this setback, the Dutch put Austria and Italy to the sword in the second round to reach consecutive World Cup finals.

The final itself was an ill-tempered match against the hosts. Argentina appeared to delay the start of the match and then their players complained about a plaster cast on René van de Kerkhof's wrist, which only allowed the tension in

the stadium to increase. Argentina opened the scoring through Mario Kempes but Dick Nanninga equalised late on for the Dutch. With only moments left, Rensenbrink had the chance to win the match but his shot cannoned off the post and the game went to extra time. Kempes and Bertoni scored again to consign the Dutch to defeat. They then refused to attend the post-match festivities.

Rensenbrink played in a few of the qualifying matches for the 1980 European Championships before retiring from international football, although he played on at domestic level with Toulouse until 1982.

**Name:** Pieter Robert 'Rob' Rensenbrink
**Born:** July 3rd 1947, Amsterdam, Netherlands
**Position:** Forward
**International Career:** 1968 – 1979
**Caps:** 46
**Goals:** 14
**Honours:** World Cup Runner-up (1974, 1978)

# Rep

Johnny Rep was another student of the Rinus Michels school of total football at Ajax in the 1970s. In five domestic seasons he scored 41 goals in 97 league appearances. He then signed for Valencia, Bastia and Saint-Étienne, and enjoyed great success in front of goal at all three clubs. He was called up for the national team before the 1974 World Cup in Germany, and he duly delivered on the biggest stage, scoring twice against Uruguay and once against Bulgaria in the first group stage, and against Argentina in the second phase. Although the Dutch initially looked like they would give the hosts a master-class in the final, the Germans ground out a 2-1 victory.

Rep was on target again at the World Cup in Argentina in 1978 but his first goal came in a shock loss to Scotland. The Netherlands squeezed through their group but then hammered Austria in the second phase with two more goals from Rep. The Dutch could only draw with archrivals West Germany but a 2-1 win over Italy saw them qualify for the final against hosts Argentina. Rob Rensenbrink had a chance to win the match in the dying seconds but his shot hit the post and Argentina scored twice in extra time to lift the trophy. Rep retired before the 1982 World Cup and moved into management in 1994.

**Name:** John Nicholaas 'Johnny' Rep
**Born:** November 25th 1951, Zaandam, Netherlands
**Position:** Right wing
**International Career:** 1973 - 1981
**Caps:** 42
**Goals:** 12
**Honours:** World Cup Runner-up (1974, 1978)

# Rijkaard

**Below:** *A young Frank Rijkaard in Ajax colours in 1981*

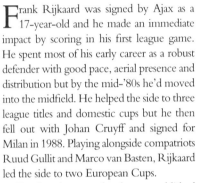

Frank Rijkaard was signed by Ajax as a 17-year-old and he made an immediate impact by scoring in his first league game. He spent most of his early career as a robust defender with good pace, aerial presence and distribution but by the mid-'80s he'd moved into the midfield. He helped the side to three league titles and domestic cups but he then fell out with Johan Cruyff and signed for Milan in 1988. Playing alongside compatriots Ruud Gullit and Marco van Basten, Rijkaard led the side to two European Cups.

By then he was already an established international in a Dutch side that went on to win the 1988 European Championships. He became involved in a bitter spat with West German striker Rudi Völler when the two clashed at Italia '90. Matches between the two nations usually descended into violence as a hangover from the German occupation during the Second World War and this encounter was fiery from the start.

Rijkaard was booked for a rash tackle on Völler and he then spat in the German's perm. Völler, inexplicably, was booked for complaining about the incident. Both men came to blows after the resulting free-kick when Völler went over in the box. The Dutch saw it as a dive and Rijkaard pulled his ear and then trod on his foot. Both men were sent off, with Rijkaard again spitting at Völler as they left the field. For a player who was normally mild-mannered, this disgusting incident is difficult to explain, although he later apologised.

This gifted, influential and versatile player was perhaps the first man since Welsh legend John Charles to be genuinely world-class in two different positions. The occasional infraction aside, he was still good enough to be selected against Brazil in the quarter-final of the 1994 World Cup. He saw out his domestic career with Ajax before moving into management, his first appointment being to the national team he'd graced only four years earlier.

---

**Name:** Franklin Edmundo 'Frank' Rijkaard
**Born:** September 30th 1962, Amsterdam, Netherlands
**Position:** Defender / midfielder
**International Career:** 1981 - 1994
**Caps:** 73
**Goals:** 10
**Honours:** European Championship Winner (1988)

---

# Rivaldo

Rivaldo began his career with Santa Cruz and over the next two decades he would develop into one of the most influential and deadly playmakers and goal-scorers in the game. He had brief spells with Mogi Mirim, Corinthians and Palmeiras before he arrived in Europe with Deportivo La Coruña. He scored 21 goals in his first 41 league matches and attracted the attention of Barcelona. He joined the Catalans in 1997, helped them to the league and cup double in his first season and scored another 86 league goals in 157 appearances. In 1999 he won another league title and was voted World Player of the Year.

He made his debut in the yellow of Brazil in 1993 and scored the only goal in a friendly against Mexico. He was blamed for their defeat at the 1996 Olympics to Nigeria, however, and coach Mário Zagallo dropped him until 1998 when he earned a recall for the World Cup in France. He helped the team reach the final but they were poor against the hosts and lost 3–0. Rivaldo made amends at the next tournament in the Far East. He scored goals in each of their first five matches and then set up Ronaldo twice in the final against Germany, but he will be remembered for an unsporting moment in the group match against Turkey when he made out that Hakan Ünsal had kicked the ball at his face when it clearly struck his thigh. He fell over theatrically and the referee sent Ünsal off. Rivaldo was later fined for his shameful performance.

He made his last appearance for the national team in 2003, although he carried on at club level with Olympiacos and AEK Athens amongst others. Despite his occasional falling out with coaches or bad sportsmanship, Rivaldo was one of the most technically gifted players of his generation. He was strong with both feet, had a surge of pace and could hold off defenders to slide crucial passes to the likes of Romário and Ronaldo.

**Above:** *Rivaldo*

| | |
|---|---|
| **Name:** | Rivaldo (Vítor Borba Ferreira) |
| **Born:** | April 19th 1972, Paulista, Brazil |
| **Position:** | Attacking midfield |
| **International Career:** | 1993 – 2003 |
| **Caps:** | 74 |
| **Goals:** | 34 |
| **Honours:** | World Cup Winner (2002) |

# Rivelino

**Right:** *Roberto Rivelino had one of the game's great left feet*

Rivelino's career began at Brazilian outfit Clube Atlético Barcelona in 1962 but he then signed for youth side Corinthians in 1963. Two years later he graduated to the senior team and he quickly developed into one of the finest midfielders in the game. With his raking long passes, thunderbolt free-kicks and silky touch, he became a fan favourite and he eventually made 471 league appearances for Corinthians. In those nine years he also scored 141 goals, but he then signed for Fluminese, where his record, if anything, improved slightly: 53 goals in 158 league starts and two championships (1975 and 1976).

A player of Rivelino's class couldn't be ignored by the national selectors and he made the first of his 92 starts for Brazil in 1965. He didn't play any part in the disastrous World Cup campaign in England the following year but he was an integral part of the all-conquering 1970 World Cup team. He scored three goals in the tournament, including a wonder free-kick against Czechoslovakia. He had less success in 1974 and 1978 in a side that clearly missed the genius of Pelé and the flair of Tostão, Gérson and Jairzinho.

He retired from international football after the World Cup in Argentina but continued his domestic career with Al-Hilal in Saudi Arabia. He hung up his boots for good in 1981 but as a player he will always be mentioned in the same breath as Zico, Sócrates and the greatest of them all, Pelé.

| | |
|---|---|
| **Name:** | Roberto Rivelino |
| **Born:** | January 1st 1946, São Paulo, Brazil |
| **Position:** | Attacking midfield |
| **International Career:** | 1965 - 1978 |
| **Caps:** | 92 |
| **Goals:** | 26 |
| **Honours:** | World Cup Winner (1970) |

# Rivera

**Above:** *Gianni Rivera*

Gianni Rivera began his career with Alessandria's youth team and he made his senior debut against Internazionale at the age of 15. After a single season he was bought by AC Milan as a replacement for Juan Schiaffino. He won his first Scudetto in 1962 and was then selected for the national squad for the World Cup in Chile. Italy missed out on qualifying from a tough group but Rivera continued his superb domestic form throughout the 1960s.

Italy won the 1968 European Championships and arrived in Mexico for the 1970 World Cup with a strong team. Offensively they failed to sparkle with Sandro Mazzola in the side so manager Ferruccio Valcareggi elected to rotate Mazzola and Rivera. The change in fortunes was dramatic: Italy beat the hosts in the quarter-final and then saw off Germany 4-3 in the semi, with Rivera scoring the extra-time winner in one of the best games in World Cup history.

Somewhat inexplicably, given that he was the catalyst for two superb performances, Valcareggi refused to start Rivera in the final against Brazil. The South Americans exploited the holes in the Italian midfield and Valcareggi compounded his tactical error by only bringing on Rivera with six minutes to go, by which time Brazil had already scored three and the game was effectively over.

He played in his fourth World Cup in 1974 but missed Italy's last game, a 2-1 loss to Poland. He retired from international football but played on with Milan until 1979, by which time he'd scored 184 goals in 744 games.

**Name:** Giovanni 'Gianni' Rivera
**Born:** August 18th 1943, Alessandria, Italy
**Position:** Midfield
**International Career:** 1962 - 1974
**Caps:** 60
**Goals:** 14
**Honours:** European Championship Winner (1968), World Cup Runner-up (1970)

# Romário

Romário began his youth career with Olaria and then Vasco da Gama, and he graduated to the latter's senior side in 1985. He wasn't a prolific goal-scorer in his first three years but a move to PSV Eindhoven saw him explode onto the world stage with 96 league goals in only 107 games in his first five seasons. He then signed for Barcelona, Flamengo and Valencia, but the goals kept coming and in his league career he would eventually score 309 in 448 games. Overall, he would become one of the few players in history to score more than 1,000 goals, although this did include 77 in friendlies and youth games.

He was voted World Player of the Year in 1994 after teaming up with strike partner Bebeto during the glorious World Cup campaign in the USA. In his later years he played alongside Ronaldo and the pair each bagged a hat-trick in the final of the 1997 Confederations Cup against Australia. He was controversially left out of the squad for the 1998 World Cup in France but he later admitted to having a muscle injury, and he was overlooked again four years later by Luiz Felipe Scolari on the grounds of indiscipline. He played his last game in the yellow of Brazil in a tribute match against Guatemala in 2005.

There can be no doubt that Romário was one of the best strikers in the game's history. His turn of pace, devastating swerve and clinical and ruthless finishing would have allowed him to play at the highest level in any era. His overall record for his country (which includes matches played at the Olympics) is bettered only by Pelé.

**Name:** Romário (de Souza Faria)
**Born:** January 29th 1966, Rio de Janeiro, Brazil
**Position:** Striker
**International Career:** 1987 - 2005
**Caps:** 85
**Goals:** 71
**Honours:** World Cup Winner (1994)

# Ronaldinho

Ronaldinho blushes when he is compared with Pelé and Zico, and, when asked by a journalist how he felt about being the best player in the world, he replied that he wasn't even the best player at Barcelona. However, such modesty cannot hide his irrepressible skills and achievements: FIFA World Player of the Year in 2004 and 2005, as well as European Player of the Year in 2005. His best position is just behind the strikers but his technical ability and flair mean he can operate anywhere in attack or midfield. In Brazil he is commonly referred to as Ronaldinho Gaúcho to distinguish himself from his namesake Ronaldo (who is already referred to as Ronaldinho or 'little Ronaldo'). Gaúcho is the name commonly used for people from the Rio Grande do Sul region of Brazil.

Ronaldo Assis de Moreira was born in a favela in Porto Alegre, Brazil on 21st March 1980. His father was a shipyard worker and stadium security guard, while his mother worked as a civil servant at the town hall. When his older brother, Roberto, started

**Above:**
*Ronaldinho*

playing professionally for one of the city's major teams, Grêmio, it provided the family with financial security. In an attempt to convince the young star not to move to Europe, the club bought the family a nice villa. It was here, tragically, that his father, João, died in an accident in the family pool when Ronaldinho was eight, so Roberto began looking after his family. His own career, however, was cut short by injury before he could reach his potential.

Before soccer, Ronaldinho loved playing futsal (a form of fast indoor five-a-side soccer) and beach football, which, in part, explains some of his exceptional close control. The youngster's prodigious talent was recognised early, with his brother taking him to Grêmio's youth set-up. He was even captured on film scoring all 23 goals in a 23-0 win. Recognition followed

**Above:**
*Ronaldinho controls the ball during the Confederations Cup*

as he starred in Brazil's Under-17 World Cup win in Egypt, where he was named as the best player in the tournament. In 1998 he made his professional debut for Grêmio and a year later he debuted for Brazil's senior team against Latvia. He then came on as a substitute in the Copa América to score an exceptional goal in a 7-0 demolition of Venezuela. Later that year he was part of the Brazilian squad in the Confederations Cup. He scored in every game but was injured for the final, which they lost 4-3 to Mexico. With his club, he scored 22 goals and helped Grêmio win the Campeonato Gaúcho (state championship) and the Copa Sul (the regional Southern Cup) in 1999. However, in 2000, his contract expired. Despite being happy at the club, he looked for a new challenge. With Europe beckoning, top

French side Paris Saint-Germain (PSG) underwent months of intense negotiations before Ronaldinho was finally allowed to leave for the bargain price of 4.5 million euros in 2001.

Ronaldinho's skills continued to develop during his two seasons at PSG but he also hit the headlines over his disciplinary problems and his partying on the Parisian nightclub scene. Even so, he still scored 68 goals and played a significant part in Brazil's 2002 World Cup victory in South Korea – including scoring the winner against England in the quarter-final with an audacious free kick before being sent off seven minutes later. Another season and more controversy followed at PSG, when he stated publicly that he wanted to move on. The elite clubs lined up for his signature and for a long time it looked like he would become a Manchester United player, but it was Barcelona who eventually paid the £20 million transfer in 2003.

At Camp Nou, Ronaldinho continued to mature as a player and a person and he became one of football's great icons. His ability to turn a match with a piece of magic made him central to Barça's recent success and won him the adoration of football fans the world over. Despite the club struggling during his first season, they went on a 17-match unbeaten run, finished second and qualified for the Champions League. They won the league the following season and Ronaldinho was voted FIFA World Player of the Year in 2004 and 2005, as well as being awarded the Ballon D'Or (European Footballer of the Year) in 2005. The club won La Liga again in 2006 and also triumphed in the Champions League final against Arsenal.

Ronaldinho was now central to Brazil's national team and led them to Confederation's Cup victory in Germany in 2005 with a 4–1 victory over Argentina. Brazil had high expectations for the 2006 World Cup but Ronaldinho was a shadow of his former self and Brazil were knocked out in the quarter-final by France. The media were quick to criticise him when he was pictured partying in Barcelona a few days later with fellow international Adriano.

He played his 200th game for Barcelona in 2007 but then transferred to AC Milan after turning down an offer from Manchester City thought to be worth £25 million. Despite his skill and extrovert lifestyle he has tried to remain close to his roots and family (brother Roberto is his manager and sister Deisi is his press coordinator). Having returned to form and been named in the 30-man provisional squad for the 2010 World Cup in South Africa, he was not in Coach Dunga's final squad of 23. Critics claim that his exclusion signals a deviation from the classic Brazilian attacking style of play, but he has recently been recalled to the side and could make it to the 2014 World Cup.

---

**Name:** Ronaldinho (Ronaldo Assis de Moreira)
**Born:** March 21st 1980, Porto Alegre, Brazil
**Position:** Attacking midfield
**International Career:** 1999 – present
**Caps:** 97
**Goals:** 33
**Honours:** World Cup Winner (2002)

---

# Ronaldo

Known as The Phenomenon (El Fenómeno in Portuguese, or O Fenômeno in Spanish), Ronaldo is regarded as one of the most dangerous strikers in the game. He had the ability to beat any defender with pace and skill but he also had great body strength and power. Having won the World Cup twice with Brazil, in 1994 and 2002, he holds the competition's all-time scoring record with 15 goals in 19 games at three World Cups (he was selected for the 1994 squad but didn't play a match, although he did score three goals at the 2006 tournament). He also won the FIFA World Player of the Year three times, in 1996, 1997 and 2002.

Ronaldo Luis Nazário de Lima was born in Bento Ribeiro, a working-class neighbourhood on the outskirts of Rio de Janeiro. Like most Brazilian children, he played football barefoot with his friends in the streets rather than go to school. His tremendous talent was spotted when he was playing for the São Cristóvão youth team by former Brazilian star, Jairzinho.

The legendary player recommended the young Ronaldo to the Brazilian national youth team and his own former club, Cruzeiro. He became a teenage prodigy for the club, scoring 12 goals in 14 league games in 1993, and was rewarded with a call-up to the Brazilian senior team at the age of 17. He made his debut against Argentina in 1994. Later that year he was a member of the World Cup-winning squad in the USA but he was taken for the experience rather than to play and he remained on the bench.

After scoring a goal in his first game of the 1994 season, Dutch giants PSV Eindhoven swooped for the youngster for a fee of £3.2 million. Critics argued it was an exorbitant amount for a teenager but Ronaldo delivered, scoring 51 goals in 53 appearances over the next two years. He helped PSV to the KNVB Beker (Dutch Cup) in 1996, beating Sparta Rotterdam 5-2 in the final, and was the league's top scorer in 1995. With growing popularity and recognition in Europe, bigger clubs soon took notice and Barcelona secured his signature for £10.25 million. It was another enormous fee that proved to be shrewd business. He topped the Primera Liga's scoring charts in the 1996-7 season with 34 goals (with 13 more in the Spanish Cup and European Cup Winners' Cup), before another move to Inter Milan for a world record £19 million. He promptly won his first World Player of the Year in 1996. Aged only 20, he was the youngest winner of the award. He then played a crucial role in Brazil's victory in the 1997 Copa América, scoring five goals as they cruised through the tournament and beat hosts Bolivia 3-1 in the final.

Ronaldo's time at Inter Milan was littered with highs and lows. He started well with 25 goals in 32 games and retained the FIFA World Player of the Year award. He also won the European Player of the Year in 1997 and scored in the 3-0 defeat of Lazio in the 1998 UEFA Cup final. He starred as Brazil fought their way to the final of the 1998 World Cup in France but audiences were surprised by his lacklustre display in the 3-0 loss to France. It emerged

**Above:** *Ronaldo*

later that he had suffered a convulsive fit on the morning of the match and had been rushed to hospital. His team-mates were clearly shaken and performed poorly. He was still awarded the Golden Ball as the tournament's best player, while Davor Šuker was awarded the Golden Boot as its top scorer for third-placed Croatia.

Brazil won the 1999 Copa América

## RONALDO

(defeating Uruguay 3-0 in the final) with Ronaldo top scoring, but he suffered a bad knee injury that ushered in a turbulent period as he struggled to regain his fitness. He ruptured a knee ligament only six minutes into his comeback match, which sidelined him for the whole of the 2000–01 season), and then a thigh strain further hampered his recovery. After nearly two years' rehabilitation, having been written off by many experts, Ronaldo returned in style at the 2002 World Cup in South Korea and Japan. As part of the 'Three Rs' (alongside Rivaldo and Ronaldinho), he was in scintillating form and finished as the tournament's top scorer. He scored the only goal against Turkey in the semi-final and notched twice in the final against Germany to give Brazil the trophy for a record fifth time. With the demons of France '98 exorcised, he revived his club career by moving to Real Madrid for another world record fee of £29 million.

As part of Los Galácticos alongside Luís Figo, Zinedine Zidane and David Beckham, he won his second European Player of the Year and third World Player of the Year awards in 2002. In his first season, he helped Real win La Liga with 23 goals in 31 matches. The following season

Real failed to retain the title but Ronaldo finished as the league's top scorer. Although the team was inconsistent, Ronaldo continued to score, but with Ramón Calderón being elected chairman in 2006 and the appointment of Fabio Capello as manager, Ronaldo was marginalised for a perceived lack of fitness, pace and form. The 2006 World Cup in Germany brought more criticism after a lacklustre start to the tournament. However, against Japan in the final group match he scored twice before breaking Gerd Müller's all-time scoring record with his 15th World Cup goal in a 3-0 victory over Ghana.

Despite scoring more than 100 goals for Real, his poor relationship with Capello led to speculation about his future and he eventually signed for AC Milan in 2007 for £5 million. This was an interesting move as it meant he'd played on both sides of two of the fiercest domestic rivalries in football: Barcelona vs Real, and Inter vs AC Milan. In 2008 he suffered a recurrence of the knee ligament problem and his contract was not renewed. He announced his retirement after two productive seasons with Corinthians in his native Brazil.

Outside football, Ronaldo's personal life has been under constant media scrutiny. Some commentators asserted that his performances reflected his level (or lack) of happiness. In 2005 he became co-owner of A1 Grand Prix Team Brazil but he has become better known for his philanthropic work. Despite the luxury lifestyle and huge sums of money earned during his career, Ronaldo hasn't forgotten his roots and uses his wealth and status to help those less fortunate. He was appointed as a United Nations Development Programme (UNDP) Goodwill Ambassador in 2000.

---

**Name:** Ronaldo (Luís Nazário de Lima)
**Born:** September 18th 1976, Rio de Janeiro, Brazil
**Position:** Striker
**International Career:** 1994 - 2011
**Caps:** 98
**Goals:** 62
**Honours:** World Cup Winner (1994, 2002)

---

# Ronaldo, Cristiano

The most skilful and exciting player of the current generation, Cristiano Ronaldo is now a global footballing superstar. He uses either foot to dribble past defenders for Real Madrid and Portugal before accelerating and shooting past the world's best goalkeepers.

Cristiano Ronaldo was born in Funchal, Madeira. He often played against older boys and by the age of 10 his exceptional talent was spotted by Sporting Lisbon. He was only 12 when he moved to the mainland to work his way through the youth teams. Aged 17, he scored twice on his first-team debut, and Manchester United's players convinced manager Sir Alex Ferguson to sign him in 2003. It was an inspired move and Ronaldo was soon lighting up the Premiership with his dazzling flair.

He earned his first Portuguese cap against Kazakhstan in 2003 and went on to become the star of the European Championships on home soil in 2004. At the 2006 World Cup, the Portuguese were criticised for their unsporting behaviour, with Ronaldo becoming public enemy number one in England after he appeared to get club-mate Wayne Rooney sent off in their clash with England.

Sir Alex Ferguson convinced Ronaldo to stay at United and he and Rooney were soon terrorising defences while winning the league in 2006-07, a year in which he also won the PFA Fans' Player of the Year, the Football Writers' Association Footballer of the Year, Barclay's Player of the Season, PFA Young Player of the Year, and PFA Player's Player of the Year. He was named in the PFA Team of the Year, as well as being the Portuguese Footballer of the Year.

In 2009 he signed for Real Madrid for a world record £80 million. In the 2010-11 season, he underlined his maturity and devastating finishing by notching an incredible 53 goals. He, club-mate Gareth Bale and Argentina and Barcelona's maestro Lionel Messi are the only players to stand head and shoulders above their contemporaries in

the game today. Ronaldo continues to improve and he scored his 230th Real Madrid goal in only his 221st appearance early in 2014.

He is equally devastating for his country and has now scored 47 times in only 109 international appearances. He is still only 28 so could enjoy another seven seasons and break countless more records if he stays fit and motivated.

**Name:** Cristiano Ronaldo (dos Santos Aveiro)
**Born:** February 5th 1985, Funchal, Madeira
**Position:** Forward
**International Career:** 2003 – present
**Caps:** 109
**Goals:** 47
**Honours:** European Championship Runner-up (2004)

**Above:** *Cristiano Ronaldo of Portugal holds his hands up during the UEFA EURO 2008 Quarter Final match between Portugal and Germany*

# Rossi

*Below: Paolo Rossi scored a hat-trick for Italy against Brazil at the 1982 World Cup*

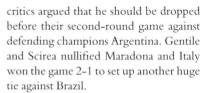

**Below:** *Paolo Rossi scored a hat-trick for Italy against Brazil at the 1982 World Cup*

Paolo Rossi was loaned out to Como from Juventus to gain experience and see whether he could recover from knee surgery to play at the highest level. In 1976, Vincenza's coach, Giovan Fabbri, decided to play him as a striker and Rossi duly delivered, scoring 60 goals in 94 league appearances and helping the team to promotion to Serie A. National coach Enzo Bearzot then picked him for the 1978 World Cup in Argentina. He scored three goals and provided several assists as Italy beat France, Hungary and hosts Argentina in the group phase. They eventually finished the tournament in fourth place after losing to Brazil.

Rossi's career looked to be going in the right direction when he was implicated in a betting scandal while at Perugia and banned for two years. He made his comeback at the 1982 World Cup but Italy were poor in the group phase and only scraped through to the knockout stages. Rossi's fitness and desire were called into question and

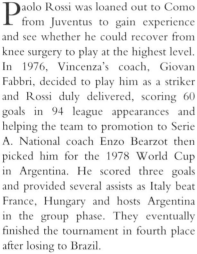

critics argued that he should be dropped before their second-round game against defending champions Argentina. Gentile and Scirea nullified Maradona and Italy won the game 2-1 to set up another huge tie against Brazil.

Rossi was inspired and scored a fabulous hat-trick, and he then netted a brace against Poland to drag Italy to the final against West Germany. He opened the scoring in the final itself and Italy eventually won 3-1. It was a remarkable turnaround for a man who'd been pilloried in the press for his anonymity in the first round.

Rossi was injured for the 1986 World Cup and he retired from domestic football the following year. He will always be remembered as the man who broke Brazilian hearts in 1982 with a performance of the highest quality that earned him the Golden Boot.

**Name:** Paolo Rossi
**Born:** September 23rd 1956, Prato, Italy
**Position:** Striker
**International Career:** 1977 - 1986
**Caps:** 48
**Goals:** 20
**Honours:** World Cup and Golden Boot Winner (1982)

# Rummenigge

Karl-Heinz Rummenigge joined the Lippstadt youth team in 1963 and Bayern Munich eventually signed him in 1974, not as an out-and-out striker but as a holding forward because of his close control and strength. Under Hungarian coach Pál Csernai, however, he developed into one of the most feared strikers in the game. He guided Bayern to the European Cup twice, although he was apparently so nervous before the 1976 final that he had to be plied with brandy. With team-mate Paul Breitner, the pair formed an alliance that was so devastating the press dubbed the side FC Breitnigge.

Rummenigge was called up to the national team after their loss in the 1976 European Championship final to Czechoslovakia. He announced himself on the biggest stage two years later at the World Cup in Argentina when he scored twice against Mexico in the first group stage. Despite scoring again in the second round against Austria, West Germany conceded a late Hans Krankl

goal and were eliminated.

By 1980 Rummenigge was at his peak: he scored against Czechoslovakia in the opening game of Euro '80 and partnered match-winner Horst Hrubesch up front in the final against Belgium. He scored four more goals in the group phase of Spain '82, which included a hat-trick against Chile, and West Germany topped their group in the second round with a win over the hosts. Rummenigge found the net again in an epic semi-final against the French, and he also scored his spot-kick in the shootout that saw the Germans through to the World Cup final. A Paolo Rossi-inspired Italy proved too strong, however.

The Germans were uncharacteristically poor during Euro '84 but Rummenigge was back to his best for the 1986 World Cup in Mexico. Although he didn't score in any of the group games or in the first three knockout matches, he popped up to score in the 74th minute of the final against Argentina

**Above:** *Karl-Heinz Rummenigge controls the ball on his chest in the 1986 World Cup final against Argentina*

to give the Germans hope. They had been 2-0 down to Maradona's side but when Rudi Völler equalised in the 80th minute it looked like the game would go to extra time. Maradona then provided a delightful through-ball for Jorge Burruchaga to score the winner six minutes from time. Rummenigge promptly retired from international football, although he played on domestically with Servette FC until 1989. His tally of 338 goals in 682 games is extremely impressive

given that he took time to develop into a lethal front man.

**Name:** Karl-Heinz Rummenigge
**Born:** September 25th 1955, Lippstadt, West Germany
**Position:** Striker
**International Career:** 1976 - 1986
**Caps:** 95
**Goals:** 45
**Honours:** European Championship Winner (1980), World Cup Runner-up (1982, 1986)

# Sánchez

Hugo Sánchez played his youth football with UNAM Pumas. He was a gifted footballer with an eye for goal and he netted 99 times in 183 league starts for the senior team between 1976 and 1981. After a short loan spell in the US he signed for Atlético Madrid and kept up his goal-every-two-games average until 1985 when he signed for Madrid's biggest side, Real. Over the next seven seasons he set scoring records aplenty (253 in just 283 games) and won five consecutive league championships. All 38 goals he scored in 1989-90 required only a single touch.

Sánchez was first selected for the Mexican national team in 1977 when he was only 19. He scored four times in three games later that year but Mexico performed poorly at the 1978 World Cup and then didn't qualify for Spain '82. Mexico hosted the 1986 World Cup and Sánchez scored in their first match against Belgium. Mexico topped their group with a win over Iraq, and they then beat Bulgaria in the round of 16. Despite drawing with eventual finalists West Germany in the quarter-final, Sánchez's team lost on penalties and were eliminated.

Mexico failed to reach Italia '90 but Sánchez's goals ensured the national team qualified for the next tournament in the USA. He scored his last goal in the 1993 Copa América but was only a peripheral player at the World Cup the following summer because of his frequent run-ins with the Mexican Football Federation. He retired from domestic football in 1997 having scored more than 400 goals in 700 appearances.

**Name:** Hugo Sánchez (Márquez)
**Born:** July 11th 1958, Mexico City, Mexico
**Position:** Striker
**International Career:** 1977 - 1994
**Caps:** 58
**Goals:** 29
**Honours:** CONCACAF Gold Cup (1977)

# Santos, Djalma

Djalma Santos began his career in the centre of defence with local club side Portuguesa. He then graduated to right back and remained there for 11 years and 434 league appearances. After only four years as a professional he was called up for the national team and he made his debut against Peru. Two years later he played in his first World Cup and helped his team demolish Mexico 5-0 in their opening match. He scored from the penalty spot in their quarter-final against Hungary but the Magnificent Magyars ran out 4-2 winners in what was subsequently called the 'Battle of Bern' because of the overt aggression shown by both sides.

Santos had been dropped in the build-up to the 1958 tournament in Sweden and he didn't play until the final. Pelé may have been the young inspiration for the team but Djalma Santos was the rock in defence. As a result of this single superb performance he was voted into the all-star team of the tournament. Brazil lifted the trophy after a 5-2 win.

Four years later he played in every game and guided the team to consecutive finals, and it was he who lobbed a difficult cross into the box for Vavá to hammer home after Viliam Schrojf had fumbled the ball. He was a surprise selection for the 1966 World Cup in England because he was now 37 and Carlos Alberto was expected to fill the right-back role. Santos played in the first two matches but was dropped after their 3-1 defeat to Hungary and subsequent elimination from the tournament. Along with Franz Beckenbauer, he is the only player to be named in the all-star team at three World Cups.

He continued his club football with Palmeiras and eventually made 498 appearances for the side. There's no doubting his defensive qualities but he also launched attacks from right back and is rated as one of the best defenders the game has ever produced.

**Name:** Djalma (Pereira Dias dos) Santos
**Born:** February 27th 1929, São Paulo, Brazil
**Position:** Right back
**International Career:** 1952 - 1968
**Caps:** 98
**Goals:** 3
**Honours:** World Cup Winner (1958, 1962)

# Santos, Nílton

Nílton Santos began his career with Botafogo and eventually made 723 league appearances for the side. He was one of a new breed of defenders who pioneered attacking runs up the line that would one day be associated with the wing-backs. He was called up to the squad for the 1950 World Cup on home soil but he didn't play in any matches and some put Brazil's defensive frailty down to his absence.

Four years later he was again in the World Cup squad but he didn't get his reward until Brazil finally won the Jules Rimet Trophy in Sweden in 1958. In their match against Austria he broke from defence early in the second half and beat almost the entire Austrian team before shooting past the helpless 'keeper. He was on hand again in the final to keep the Swedes at bay.

He lifted the World Cup for the second time in Chile in 1962 but, at 37, he was past his best and slipped into retirement as possibly the finest attacking left back in the game's history.

**Left:** *Nílton Santos*

**Name:** Nílton (dos) Santos
**Born:** May 16th 1925, Rio de Janeiro, Brazil
**Position:** Left back
**International Career:** 1945 – 1962
**Caps:** 75
**Goals:** 3
**Honours:** World Cup Winner (1958, 1962)

# Schmeichel

The Great Dane is rated by players and fans alike as the finest goalkeeper of the last 20 years. Despite only receiving a wildcard to enter the 1992 European Championships in Sweden, he led Denmark to the title, beating the mighty Germans (then world champions) in the final. Having moved to Manchester United, he was the driving force behind a defence that kept out all-comers and allowed the side to complete a remarkable treble (League Championship, FA Cup and European Cup) in 1999.

Peter Schmeichel was born in Gladsaxe, Denmark, in November 1963. He played his first match just before his ninth birthday and was soon approached by the Gladsaxe Hero youth team coach. He graduated to the senior squad in his late teens and met mentor Svend Hansen. The coach played him in a big match straight away and Schmeichel's performance was praised by the local press.

Hansen then helped him map out his career and he joined Hvidovre in 1985. His side was relegated but Schmeichel had been spotted by Brøndby's scouts and he was signed in 1987. The team won the Danish league in his first season and Schmeichel was soon called up for Denmark. He impressed immediately and was promoted to number one in time for the 1988 European Championships, although the national team couldn't build on his solid performances.

Domestically, Brøndby were unstoppable, winning four league titles and reaching the semi-final of the UEFA Cup. It was only a matter of time before the giants of Europe came looking for a superstar goalkeeper and he was bought by Manchester United for half a million pounds, a price that turned out to be the bargain of the century. United were runners-up in his first season but they won the League Cup for the first time in the club's history.

By now, Schmeichel was becoming the dominant goalkeeping force on the continent. At the 1992 European Championships in Sweden, the Danes battled through to a semi-final spot against

the much-fancied holders, the Netherlands. The match went to penalties and Schmeichel made the decisive save from Marco van Basten. Denmark were criticised for their negative tactics in a dour final against Germany but they scored twice and Schmeichel kept them in the match with marvellous saves from Jürgen Klinsmann, Thomas Häßler and Stefan Effenberg.

At Euro '96 Denmark were eliminated in the group stage but they performed well at France '98 and were only knocked out by Brazil (3-2) in a tight quarter-final. He was known for his ability to pop up in the opposition penalty area if his side was behind and he scored several goals, including an international spot-kick against Belgium in 2000. The side was eliminated from Euro 2000 at the group stage and Schmeichel announced his international retirement the following February.

He spent the best years of his club career at Manchester United and the side won five Premier League titles, three FA Cups, a League Cup, and the Champions League against Bayern Munich in Barcelona. He then moved briefly to Sporting Lisbon in Portugal before returning to the Premier League with Aston Villa and Manchester City. Having retired, he worked for the BBC and Danish television.

Allying his fearsome reputation with superb technique and determination, Schmeichel pulled off the spectacular and the regulation with consummate ease, and he set the standard by which all modern goalkeepers are measured.

---

**Name:** Peter Boleslaw Schmeichel
**Born:** November 18th 1963, Gladsaxe, Denmark
**Position:** Goalkeeper
**International Career:** 1987 - 2001
**Caps:** 129
**Goals:** 1
**Honours:** European Championship Winner (1992)

# Scifo

**Below:** *Belgium's Enzo Scifo tries to dispossess Maradona in the semi-final of the 1986 World Cup*

How Scifo would have relished playing in the current Belgium team alongside such gifted players like Simon Mignolet, Jan Vertonghen, Thomas Vermaelen, and a host of others plying their trade in the Premier League. That Scifo made an ordinary team into a good one by lifting team-mates who weren't as technically proficient to his level is testament to his outstanding ability.

Scifo earned the nickname 'Little Pelé' with his youth team and he signed for RSC Anderlecht as a teenager in 1982. He made his senior debut the following season and, over the next five years, he scored 32 league goals in 119 appearances. He then transferred to Internazionale but didn't enjoy much success there or with Bordeaux so he signed for Auxerre in 1989. This move revitalised his domestic career and he joined Torino in 1991.

Scifo made his debut for the national side aged just 18. He went on to play in four World Cups, the first of which was in Mexico in 1986. The Belgians lost their opening game to the hosts but a Scifo strike helped them overcome Iraq in their next match. A 2-2 draw with Paraguay saw them squeeze through into the knockout phase. Scifo was on target again as Belgium overcame the Soviet Union 4-3, and he scored his penalty to see off Spain in the quarter-final. Scifo was a gifted playmaker with great vision but he couldn't compete with Maradona's Argentina in the semi-final and Belgium had to be content with fourth place after defeat to France in the playoff.

Belgium beat South Korea and Uruguay in the group stage of the 1990 World Cup but a wonder goal from England's David Platt saw them knocked out in the round of 16. Two more group-stage wins at USA '94 saw them face Germany in the round of 16, and the Belgians were again narrowly defeated, 3-2. Scifo played the last of his 16 World Cup games in France in 1998. It's no coincidence that the autumn of his career mirrored a decline in the national side's fortunes and Belgium failed to escape their group after three draws. Scifo moved into management in 2001 and has so far taken charge at four clubs.

**Name:** Vincenzo Daniele 'Enzo' Scifo
**Born:** February 19th 1966, Haine-Saint-Paul, Belgium
**Position:** Attacking midfielder
**International Career:** 1984 - 1998
**Caps:** 84
**Goals:** 18
**Honours:** UEFA Cup Runner-up (1982, 1992)

# Seeler

U we Seeler played almost his entire career for Hamburger SV. He'd joined the youth team in 1946 and made his debut for the senior side eight years later against Holstein Kiel in a cup match. His prolific scoring saw him selected for the national team in 1954 but he wasn't picked for the World Cup squad and so didn't receive a winners' medal.

Seeler scored his first international goals in 1958 and helped his side to the semi-final of the World Cup. He was on target against Argentina and Northern Ireland in the group stage but he couldn't add to his tally as West Germany lost to France in the playoff for third place.

He was at the peak of his powers four years later in Chile and his goals helped West Germany overcome Switzerland and the hosts in their group. They were then beaten by a strong Yugoslavian side in the quarter-final and it seemed as if Seeler wouldn't get the rewards his talent merited.

West Germany made it to the World Cup final in England in 1966 after wins over Switzerland, Spain, Uruguay and the Soviet Union. Despite losing the match 4-2, and being pictured leaving the field utterly dejected in one of the most famous sports photos of all time, Seeler was named in the team of the tournament.

He only managed one more international goal in his next seven appearances and was a doubt for the World Cup in Mexico in 1970, but, having been selected (as captain), he delivered again, becoming the first person to score in four tournaments (beating Pelé by a few minutes) and the only player to score at least two goals in each of his four World Cups. He opened the scoring in a 2-1 win over Morocco, and scored again against Bulgaria and England. West Germany eventually finished third after being knocked out by Italy (4-3) in a thrilling semi-final.

Seeler was unlucky not to have lifted the World Cup but his 500+ top-flight goals, 21 matches at the finals themselves, four successive World Cup tournaments and exceptional strike rate for the national team elevate him to the game's elite.

---

**Name:** Uwe Seeler
**Born:** November 5th 1936, Hamburg, Germany
**Position:** Striker
**International Career:** 1954 - 1970
**Caps:** 72
**Goals:** 43
**Honours:** World Cup Runner-up (1966)

---

# Stábile

Guillermo Stábile started his career with Sportivo Metán before joining Huracán in 1920. Four years later he graduated into the top flight and moved from wide on the flank to the central striker's role. He won two national championships with the side and also a regional trophy in 1925. His prolific marksmanship in front of goal (102 in only 119 club games) brought him to the attention of the national team and he was selected for the first World Cup in Uruguay in 1930.

He didn't start Argentina's first match against France but came on against Mexico in the second game and scored what for three quarters of a century was thought to be the first World Cup hat-trick. It was later discovered, however, that American Bert Patenaude scored three against Paraguay two days earlier. Stábile scored another two against Chile in the final group game and took his team to a semi-final against the United States. Stábile notched another brace in a 6-1 demolition of their opponents and Argentina were in the World Cup final.

Stábile put Argentina 2-1 up against Uruguay but the hosts fought back to take the match 4-2. Despite the defeat, Stábile made history by being the first winner of the Golden Boot for scoring the most goals in the tournament: eight in just four matches. For reasons that aren't understood, he was never selected by his country again. Instead, he turned his considerable talents to managing the national side and guided them to six South American Championships. He ended a magnificent managerial career with 83 victories from 123 games.

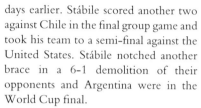

**Name:** Guillermo Stábile
**Born:** January 17th 1905, Buenos Aires, Argentina
**Died:** December 26th 1966, Buenos Aires
**Position:** Striker
**International Career:** 1930
**Caps:** 4
**Goals:** 8
**Honours:** World Cup Golden Boot (1930)

# Stoichkov

**Above:** *Hristo Stoichkov celebrates another goal for Bulgaria*

Hristo Stoichkov began playing for his local club before moving to Hebros in 1982. A move to domestic giants CSKA Sofia followed two years later and his ability in front of goal (81 league goals in 119 starts) brought him to the attention of Barcelona. Johan Cruyff bought him to complete a dream team and Stoichkov delivered again, netting 77 times in 151 league appearances over the next five seasons. He also helped the Catalans to four league titles and the European Cup.

Stoichkov was so good that he made an ordinary Bulgarian team into one that could challenge for honours on the world stage. He led them to victories over Greece and Argentina in the group stage of the 1994 World Cup, and then Mexico and Germany in the knockout phase. Their remarkable run was finally ended by the Italians in the semi-final and a demoralised team was then thrashed 4-0 by Sweden in the playoff for third place. His six goals earned him the Golden Boot, however. He scored another 10 during qualifying for Euro '96 and three at the tournament itself, but he couldn't help the team progress from their group. Bulgaria were also poor at France '98 so he retired from international football the following year.

He was a combative and aggressive footballer who gained a reputation for bullying opponents and referees but his crossing, shooting and dribbling marked him out as a very special player. Indeed, his 341 goals in 696 games elevate him to the elite level of world football. Having retired from the domestic game, he briefly managed the national team and CSKA.

---

**Name:** Hristo Stoichkov
**Born:** February 8th 1966, Plovdiv, Bulgaria
**Position:** Forward
**International Career:** 1987 - 1999
**Caps:** 83
**Goals:** 37
**Honours:** World Cup All-Star Team and Golden Boot (1994)

---

# Šuker

**Right:** *Croatia's golden striker, Davor Šuker*

Davor Šuker began his club career with Osijek in 1984. In 1989 he signed for Dinamo Zagreb and netted 34 times in his first two seasons, which brought him to the attention of the national selectors. He then enjoyed six productive years with Sevilla before a big-money move to Real Madrid.

He was picked for the 1990 World Cup in Italy but didn't play in any of the matches for Yugoslavia. Shortly afterwards, he chose to represent the newly founded Croatian national team instead. He scored 12 goals in 10 qualifying matches for Euro '96 and then chipped Peter Schmeichel with an outrageous lob at the tournament itself. He was also on scintillating form during qualifying for the World Cup in France in 1998, and he continued this in the tournament proper, scoring six goals in seven matches.

Šuker opened the scoring in the semi-final against the hosts but a Lilian Thuram brace saw them eliminated. Croatia rounded off a memorable tournament by beating the Netherlands in the playoff, a remarkable achievement for a team at its first World Cup. Šuker won the Golden Boot as the top scorer and was named in the team of the tournament. The side failed to qualify for Euro 2000 and Šuker only played an hour of their 2002 World Cup match against Mexico, after which he retired.

**Name:** Davor Šuker
**Born:** January 1st 1968, Osijek, Yugoslavia
**Position:** Striker
**International Career:** 1990 – 2002
**Caps:** 71
**Goals:** 46
**Honours:** World Cup Third Place and Golden Boot (1998)

# Sükür

**Above:** *Hakan Sükür*

Hakan Sükür graduated from the Sakaryaspor youth side to the senior squad in 1987. He scored a goal every two games before joining Bursaspor for two seasons in 1990. Although he couldn't maintain his prolific goal-scoring, he was signed by domestic giants Galatasaray and still netted 54 times in 90 league appearances.

His performances earned him a call-up to the national team and he scored his first goal for Turkey in a 2-1 friendly win over Denmark. Although he scored three times during Turkey's qualifying campaign for USA '94, the side failed to make the finals. Euro '96 was also a disappointing tournament in that the Turks lost all three of their group matches. Despite scoring eight goals during qualifying for France '98 – which included a hat-trick against Wales and the winner against the Netherlands – Turkey could only finish third in their group.

Sükür therefore had to wait until 2002 to make his first appearance at the World Cup finals, but Turkey were the surprise package of the tournament. They narrowly lost to Brazil in their opening match but a 3-0 win over China saw them squeeze through their group on goal difference. This left them with a relatively easy route to the semi-final and they duly beat Japan and Senegal before again losing narrowly to eventual champions Brazil. Turkey won the unpopular third-place playoff against co-hosts South Korea, 3-2. It was in this match that he scored the fastest ever goal at the finals after only 11 seconds.

After guiding Turkey to Euro 2008, Sükür was left out of the squad for the tournament itself and promptly retired. Such was his influence on the national side that they only lost four matches in which he scored over a 15-year period. He played on for a final domestic season with Galatasaray and ended his career with 383 goals in 821 appearances.

**Name:** Hakan Sükür
**Born:** September 1st 1971, Adapazarl, Turkey
**Position:** Striker
**International Career:** 1992 - 2007
**Caps:** 112
**Goals:** 51
**Honours:** World Cup Third Place (2002)

# Tostão

Tostão once scored 47 goals in a single game while at school but he began his professional career with América in 1962. It wasn't until he signed for Cruzeiro the following year that he announced himself on the world stage, however. In the next seven seasons he made 378 league appearances and scored an incredible 249 goals.

He played a small part in the disappointing World Cup in England in 1966 but by 1970 he was at his peak. He combined the striking role with that of playmaker and allowed the likes of Pelé, Jairzinho and Rivelino to feed off his precise passing and delicate touches. He chipped in with two goals as Brazil dominated the event and cemented their status as the greatest team in history with a 4-1 demolition of Italy in the final.

He would surely have gone on to greater domestic heights and may have won the World Cup again had he not suffered a recurrence of a detached retina (he'd been hit hard in the face by a ball in 1969) in 1972. After a final season with

Vasco da Gama he was forced to retire at only 26, denying the football world one of its leading lights.

**Name:** Tostão (Eduardo Gonçalves de Andrade)
**Born:** January 25th 1947, Belo Horizonte, Brazil
**Position:** Striker
**International Career:** 1966 - 1972
**Caps:** 54
**Goals:** 32
**Honours:** World Cup Winner (1970)

# Valderrama

**Above:** *Carlos Valderrama was as famous for his haircut as he was for his elegant football*

Carlos Valderrama began his domestic career with Unión Magdalena in 1981. He spent three years with his local side before signing for Millonarios for a season, but he then spent three successful years with Deportivo Cali. A move to Montpelier in France didn't bring the success his skill deserved and he then flitted between several clubs before heading for the MLS in North America.

Valderrama was a gifted midfield playmaker whose skill was matched both by his flamboyance on the ball and his outrageous Afro haircut, which made him one of the most recognisable players in the game's history. He first played for his country in 1985 but Colombia didn't qualify for the 1986 World Cup and it wasn't until Italia '90 that the wider world was treated to his trademark dribbles and flicks. He captained the side to victory over the United Arab Emirates, and a 1-1 draw with West Germany saw the side through to the knockout phase. A Roger Milla-inspired Cameroon proved too strong in the round of 16 but Valderrama was back on centre stage four years later in the USA.

It was not a good tournament for Colombia, however. Despite beating Switzerland 2-0, an Andrés Escobar own goal against the hosts saw Colombia eliminated. Escobar was gunned down on his return home, supposedly because the goal had contributed to gambling losses by the drug cartels. Valderrama was still captain four years later for the World Cup in France, but the side was eliminated after losing 2-1 to England. Valderrama played on domestically in the US until 2002.

**Name:** Carlos Alberto Valderrama (Palacio)
**Born:** September 2nd 1961, Santa Marta, Colombia
**Position:** Midfield
**International Career:** 1985 - 1998
**Caps:** 111
**Goals:** 11
**Honours:** South American Footballer of the Year (1987, 1993)

# Van Basten

If he hadn't succumbed to injury during his prime, Marco van Basten would now be talked of as one of the game's true legends. Indeed, he was still one of the most feared strikers in history. He was agile, strong, good in the air, possessed flawless technique and was tactically astute, and he always raised his game for the big occasion. He was one of a rare breed who also enjoyed success as a manager.

Marcel van Basten was born in October 1964 in Utrecht. Aged seven, he began his football career with local club UVV, although his parents believed he would become a gymnast. Ten years later he joined Elinkwijk and his potential was soon spotted by scouts from Ajax, a club he joined in 1981. His debut was as a substitute for Johan Cruyff and he promptly scored his first senior goal. His rise continued unabated and he was the league's top scorer between 1984 and 1987, which earned him a call-up for the national team.

The 1988 European Championships in West Germany saw Van Basten at his best. He scored a hat-trick against England, the winner against the hosts in the semi-final, and an unforgettable volley to beat the Soviet Union in the final. His performances gained him worldwide attention and he was lured to Italian giants AC Milan. Although the side won the Serie A title, his first season was marred by recurring ankle injuries. The following season, he was fully fit, scored 32 goals, and guided the side to European Cup victory over Steaua Bucharest. They defended the trophy the following year against Benfica.

Van Basten had a poor World Cup in 1990 and his form also slipped domestically after arguments with manager Arrigo Sacchi. In 1992, Fabio Capello took over at AC and a revitalised Van Basten helped the club to the title in an unbeaten season. His upsurge in form carried over to the Dutch national team and they reached the semi-final of Euro

'92 in Sweden but the tournament's surprise package, Denmark, knocked them out on penalties.

The following season, he was named FIFA and World Soccer Magazine's Player of the Year but the old ankle injury returned and curtailed a brilliant career. His last appearance came in AC Milan's Champions League final defeat by Olympique de Marseille. Having claimed to be retiring from all forms of football, he surprised many by being lured into management, and in 2003 he became assistant manager for the Ajax second team. In another controversial move, he was named as the manager of the Dutch national team the following year.

Van Basten shook up an under-achieving squad and took them to the knockout stages of the 2006 World Cup in Germany where they eventually lost to Portugal, his first competitive defeat as manager. He promptly resigned and took over at Ajax and then at Heerenveen, although he still occasionally works as a television pundit.

**Above:** *Holland's Marco van Basten*

**Name:** Marcel 'Marco' van Basten
**Born:** October 31st 1964, Utrecht, Netherlands
**Position:** Striker
**International Career:** 1983 - 1992
**Caps:** 58
**Goals:** 24
**Honours:** European Championship Winner (1988)

# Van Hanegem

Wim van Hanegem began his career at the age of 18 with Velox SC. He then had a brief but successful spell with Zerxes (32 league goals in 67 games) before signing for Feyenoord in 1968. Over the next eight seasons he scored a goal every three games for the domestic giants.

Van Hanegem was part of the fabulous Dutch side of the 1970s that pioneered the total football style. Each player was so comfortable on the ball that they could interchange positions to confuse their opponents. The Netherlands brushed aside Uruguay and Bulgaria in the first group stage, and then Argentina, East Germany and World Champions Brazil in the second phase.

The Dutch were tipped to overcome West Germany in a grudge final, and they duly scored from the penalty spot before the Germans had touched the ball. Van Hanegem was known for his abrasive but passionate style against the old enemy (his father and brother were killed when their shelter was targeted by German forces in 1944), and he vowed to humiliate them in the final. Unfortunately, Franz Beckenbauer lifted his side and the West Germans eventually ground out a 2-1 win. Van Hanegem was so distraught that he left the field in tears and was inconsolable for hours afterwards.

He retired from the national team in 1979 and from domestic football in 1983 after a second spell with Feyenoord. He moved into management in 1990 with USV Holland and retired for good after leaving FC Utrecht in 2008.

**Name:** Willem 'Wim' van Hanegem
**Born:** February 20th 1944, Breskens, Netherlands
**Position:** Central midfield
**International Career:** 1968 - 1979
**Caps:** 52
**Goals:** 6
**Honours:** World Cup Runner-up (1974)

# Vavá

Vavá was the world's best striker in the early 1950s. He'd joined Sport Recife in 1949 but then spent seven years with Vasco da Gama. He moved to Europe to join Atlético Madrid in 1958 and scored 31 league goals in 71 appearances over three seasons. He was called up to the national team in the wake of the disappointing performance at the 1954 World Cup and he made his mark at the next tournament in Sweden.

He scored five goals and helped Brazil to emphatic wins over France in the semi-final (5-2) and the hosts by the same score in the final. Four years later he became the first person to score in two World Cup finals when he netted in the dying moments against Czechoslovakia to secure a 3-1 win. Only three other players have since achieved this remarkable feat: Pelé scored in the 1958 and 1970 finals; Paul Breitner in 1974 and 1982; and Zinedine Zidane in 1998 and 2006.

With his diminutive stature but steel-like physique, and his turn of pace and deadly accuracy in front of goal, Vavá is

**Left:** *Vavá competes for the ball during the 1962 World Cup*

one of the all-time great centre forwards. He played on at domestic level until 1969 and then took over as manager of Córdoba, Granada and Al Rayyan. In 1985 he retired for good, a legend in his own lifetime.

**Name:** Vavá (Edvaldo Izídio Neto)
**Born:** November 12th 1934, Recife, Brazil
**Died:** January 19th 2002, Rio de Janeiro
**Position:** Striker
**International Career:** 1955 - 1964
**Caps:** 20
**Goals:** 15
**Honours:** World Cup Winner (1958, 1962)

# Villa

Nicknamed 'The Kid' on account of his youthful looks, Villa has broken just about every scoring record since he started playing with Sporting de Gijon. A big-money move to Barcelona and unparalleled success with the Spanish national side have confirmed his place at the peak of the world game alongside the likes of Argentina's Lionel Messi and Portugal's Cristiano Ronaldo.

David Villa Sánchez was born in December 1981 in northern Spain. Aged four he broke his right leg but his father managed the injury so well that by the time he recovered he could use both feet equally. Despite becoming disheartened at a lack of success in his teens, he joined the Mareo football school at 17. Sporting gave him his big break and he repaid them with 40 goals in two seasons. He then moved to Real Zaragoza and his goals helped them win the Copa del Rey, which earned him a call-up to the national squad. A move to Valencia in 2005

was all the more noticeable because he made a habit of beating the giants of Barcelona and Real Madrid.

His first international tournament was the 2006 World Cup in Germany. He and fellow striker Fernando Torres guided Spain to the knockout stages but they were eventually beaten by France. The tone had been set for Spanish domination, however, and, by the 2008 European Championships, Villa and co finally realised their potential.

Although he was injured in the semi-final, Villa's goals brought him the Golden Boot and Spain the trophy, their first international silverware. He was on target again in the build-up to the 2010 World Cup in South Africa, scoring seven in their qualifying matches to help Spain to a perfect record of 10 wins, no draws and no defeats. The tournament itself began badly with defeat to Switzerland but it was a temporary blip and he was back to his best against Portugal and

Paraguay. He was relatively quiet in the final against the brutal Dutch but Spain lifted the trophy and Villa was presented with the Silver Shoe and a place in the team of the tournament. He scored his record 50th international goal during Spain's impressive qualifying performances before the 2012 European Championships.

A move to Barcelona was somewhat inevitable given his precocious talent and he joined the Catalans for £35 million in 2010. Along with superstars like Lionel Messi, he helped Barça become all-but invincible and they won La Liga and the Champions League in 2011. In September he broke his leg in a club match and missed most of the following season and the European Championships. He returned to the national side and scored a hat-trick against Saudi Arabia, but he then made a surprising move to Atlético Madrid. If he can stay fit, he should make the squad for the 2014 World Cup.

**Above:** *David Villa of Spain runs with the ball during the FIFA 2010 World Cup*

**Name:** David Villa (Sánchez)
**Born:** December 3rd 1981, Langreo, Spain
**Position:** Striker
**International Career:** 2005 – present
**Caps:** 92
**Goals:** 56
**Honours:** European Championship Winner (2008), World Cup Winner (2010)

# Walter

Fritz Walter was one of very few top-class players to stay at one club for his entire career. He first played for Kaiserslautern as a youth in 1928 and joined the senior side in 1937. Over the next 22 years he racked up 411 league appearances and scored 380 goals. West German national coach Sepp Herberger gave him his debut against Romania in 1940 and Walter repaid the faith by scoring a hat-trick.

Walter was drafted during the war but he was captured and saw out the conflict in a prisoner-of-war camp in Hungary. When the Soviet army liberated the camp, most prisoners were taken to the gulags and worked to death but one of the guards had seen Walter play for Germany and he managed to convince the Russians not to deport him.

Walter returned to Germany and led Kaiserslautern to the domestic championship in 1951, whereupon Herberger recalled him to the national team as captain. He and his brother Ottmar were in the squad that was thrashed 8-3 by the Hungarians in the opening phase of the 1954 World Cup, but

Herberger had played a weakened team to save his stars for the knockout stages. Despite this, the Germans were still expected to lose when they met the Magnificent Magyars again in the final. Hungary went 2-0 up but a goal from Morlock and two from Rahn gave the Germans the unlikeliest of victories against a team that was on a 32-match unbeaten streak and held the highest ranking ever achieved by an international team.

Walter played his last match for West Germany in the semi-final of the 1958 World Cup against hosts Sweden. He was injured in the match and the Germans lost 3-1. They also lost the playoff to a Just Fontaine-inspired France. In 2006, on the fourth anniversary of his death, the United States played Italy at the Fritz-Walter-Stadion in Kaiserslautern after observing a minute's silence for the great man.

**Name:** Friedrich 'Fritz' Walter
**Born:** October 31st 1920, Kaiserslautern, Germany
**Died:** June 17th 2002, Enkenbach-Alsenborn, Germany
**Position:** Forward
**International Career:** 1940 - 1958
**Caps:** 61
**Goals:** 33
**Honours:** World Cup Winner (1954)

# Yashin

**Above:** *Lev Yashin*

Lev Yashin was born into a working-class family – he was forced into the factories aged 12 to help with the war effort. He joined the factory football team and was so adept in goal that he was asked to play for the Dynamo Moscow youth side. His debut in 1950 was forgettable in that the opposition keeper scored from a clearance, and he only played another two games in the next three years. He briefly thought about taking up ice hockey but regained his football form and was selected for the national team in 1954.

Four years later, Yashin was inspirational as the Soviet Union reached the quarter-final of the World Cup in Sweden. Although they lost their group match against Brazil (2-0), he was sensational and but for him the side would have been humiliated. He was selected for the All-Star Team of the Tournament. He couldn't repeat his heroics in 1962 and several poor performances saw the doubters predicting the end of his career. These predictions turned out to be somewhat premature:

Yashin led the Soviet Union to fourth place at the 1966 World Cup and, as both assistant and reserve keeper, to the quarter-final in 1970.

His 1971 testimonial in Moscow drew 100,000 spectators and players of the calibre of Pelé, Eusébio and Franz Beckenbauer. The Black Panther (on account of his favoured strip) is the only goalkeeper to be named European Footballer of the Year. He is also credited with introducing quick throws to launch counter-attacks and punching balls he knew he couldn't catch, developing a sweeping role when the defenders were unable to retreat, and saving more than 150 penalties in a glittering domestic and international career. He then beat Dino Zoff and Gordon Banks to be voted the best goalkeeper of the 20th century.

**Name:** Lev Ivanovich Yashin
**Born:** October 22nd 1929, Moscow, Soviet Union
**Died:** March 20th 1990, Moscow
**Position:** Goalkeeper
**International Career:** 1954 - 1970
**Caps:** 78
**Goals:** 0
**Honours:** Olympic Gold Medal (1956), European Championship Winner (1960)

# Zagallo

Mário Zagallo began his career with América in 1948 but he only stayed for one season before joining Flamengo. In the next eight years he scored 30 goals in 217 league appearances and was selected for the national team at the 1958 World Cup in Sweden. Zagallo played in the three group games against Austria, England and the Soviet Union, and he then scored in the final to help Brazil to a 5-2 win over the hosts. The next tournament in Chile four years later was equally successful and Zagallo scored in the opening match against Mexico. He was ever-present in the side that lifted the trophy for the second time. He retired from the national team two years later to concentrate on a coaching career.

In 1970 he became the first person to win the World Cup as a player and as a manager when he guided Brazil to glory in Mexico. Twenty-four years later he was assistant coach when Brazil won again in the USA. He was back in the top job at France '98 and led Brazil to the final, although a team shocked by

Ronaldo's earlier seizure were beaten by the hosts 3-0.

**Name:** Mário (Jorge Lobo) Zagallo
**Born:** August 9th 1931, Maceió, Brazil
**Position:** Wing
**International Career:** 1958 - 1964
**Caps:** 33
**Goals:** 5
**Honours:** World Cup Winner (1958, 1962), World Cup-Winning Coach (1970)

# Zico

Unlike many of his contemporaries, Zico came from a middle-class background rather than the favelas. He wanted to have trials with América where his brothers were playing but family friend Celso Garcia suggested he try out for Flamengo. He was slightly built so he had to bulk up but he then scored 81 goals in 116 appearances for the youth team and was promptly promoted to the professional ranks.

Zico was an inspiration with his deft touch, razor-sharp passing, turn of pace and free-kick mastery and he guided Flamengo to four national titles. He was called up for the 1978 World Cup in Argentina and looked to have secured a 2-1 win over Sweden when Welsh referee Clive Thomas disallowed his late header. Zico put a disappointing tournament behind him and, four years later in Spain, he scored four fabulous goals and created several more for a supremely talented team. However, Paolo Rossi's hat-trick in the second phase saw them eliminated.

After 212 league appearances and 123 goals for Flamengo he joined Udinese. In two seasons he struck 22 league goals but tax problems forced him to return to Brazil. He saw out his domestic career with Flamengo and then Kashima Antlers, and he was always a prolific scorer. (His 508 goals in 731 matches in all competitions for Flamengo remain records.)

At the 1986 World Cup in Mexico he played through the pain barrier after a horror tackle from Bangu's Marcio Nunes in a domestic game almost ended his career. He wasn't at his best and missed a penalty against France that would have seen Brazil progress to the semi-final. He scored his spot-kick in the resulting shootout but Sócrates and Júlio César missed theirs and Brazil were eliminated.

He retired as one of the all-time great number tens with Pelé's praise ringing in his ears: "The one player who came closest to me was Zico."

Zico has since managed, amongst others, Japan, CSKA Moscow and Olympiacos. In 2011 he took the coaching role with the Iraqi team.

**Above:** *Zico celebrates a goal with Sócrates at the 1982 World Cup*

**Name:** Zico (Arthur Antunes Coimbra)
**Born:** March 3rd 1953, Rio de Janeiro, Brazil
**Position:** Attacking midfield
**International Career:** 1976 - 1988
**Caps:** 72
**Goals:** 52
**Honours:** World Cup Squad (1978, 1982, 1986)

# Zidane

The finest footballer of his generation, Zidane guided an underperforming French team to the World Cup final in 1998, the European Championship in 2000 and a second World Cup final in 2006. Despite his exit for head-butting Marco Matterazzi in the final, he was voted the tournament's best player.

Zidane was born in Marseille in June 1972 to Algerian parents. He grew up in a small apartment in the city and learned to play football in the Place Tartane, which doubled as the block's plaza. When he was 10 he joined local side US Saint-Henri before graduating to the French Football Academy. A scout from Cannes spotted him and he made his professional debut in 1989 against Nantes. He had to wait two years for his first goal, which came against the same club, and he remained with Cannes until he was 18 before signing for Bordeaux. He enjoyed moderate success and helped them to the Intertoto Cup in 1995 but a £3-million-pound move to European Champions Juventus soon followed. The Italians won back-to-back domestic championships but lost out in two European Cup finals. He was banned for head-butting Hamburg's Jochen Kientz but was still voted the best foreign player in Serie A.

International success soon followed. Zidane made his debut against the Czech Republic in 1994 and scored both his country's goals. They were knocked out on penalties by the Czechs in the 1996 European Championships but the side was developing nicely and was expected to do well on home soil at the 1998 World Cup. In a recurring theme, the tournament was characterised by brilliance and stupidity from the mercurial playmaker: France won all of their group matches but he was sent off against Saudi Arabia for stamping on an opponent. He was suspended for the next match but then helped the French beat Italy and Croatia to land a place in the final against Brazil. Zidane scored twice and Emmanuel Petit sealed their emphatic win. Zidane was outstanding in the European Championships two years later and was again named player of the tournament.

He became the world's most expensive footballer when he was bought by Real Madrid for £50 million in 2001. Real won the 2002 Champions League final and La Liga in 2002-03, and Zidane was voted World Player of the Year for the third time. He also collected the award for being the finest European player of the previous half century.

A strong French team with many of the players that had won the previous two major tournaments was expected to perform at the World Cup in 2002 but they played terribly and were dumped out in the group stage having failed to score a goal. They were below par again at the European Championships in 2004 and were knocked out by Greece, after which Zidane announced his retirement from the national side. He was persuaded to reconsider when a number of key players failed to make the 2006 World Cup squad. Zidane promptly guided them to the final with convincing displays against Spain, Brazil and Portugal.

He was presented with the Golden Ball before the final against Italy and duly opened the scoring with a penalty, but Italy equalised and the game went to extra time. With only 10 minutes left, Zidane head-butted Marco Matterazzi and was sent off. It was a sad end to a glittering career spanning 17 years as France then lost the penalty shootout. He is now a special advisor to the Real Madrid team.

**Left:** *The mercurial Zinedine Zidane*

**Name:** Zinedine Yazid Zidane
**Born:** June 23rd 1972, Marseille, France
**Position:** Attacking midfield
**International Career:** 1994 - 2006
**Caps:** 108
**Goals:** 31
**Honours:** World Cup Winner (1998), European Championship Winner (2000), World Cup Runner-up (2006)

# Zoff

A cool and confident goalkeeper of exceptional ability, Dino Zoff was a colossus between the sticks for Juventus and Italy in the 1970s and early '80s. He is the oldest winner of the World Cup, which he lifted as Italy's captain after Spain '82.

Zoff was born in February 1942 in the provincial town of Mariano del Friuli in northern Italy. Despite his goalkeeping aspirations, he was rejected by Inter Milan and Juventus for being too short and thin so he trained as a mechanic while playing for Marianese. He was soon spotted by an Udinese scout but he only made a few appearances before moving to Mantova in 1963. He quickly established himself as a reliable shot-stopper in the first team and after 93 appearances he moved to Napoli.

He made his international debut in the qualifying matches for 1968 European Championship against Bulgaria. His side then won the trophy on home soil after beating the Soviet Union in the semi-final (on the toss of a coin after the

match ended 0-0) and Yugoslavia after a replayed final. He went on to play 112 times for his country, and also kept a record 12 consecutive clean sheets in a period when the national team began to show its potential. Italy finished fourth at both the 1978 World Cup and 1980 European Championships. Then, at the age of 40, his side finally took the sport's greatest prize, beating giants Argentina, Brazil and West Germany on the way to the World Cup in 1982.

On the domestic front, Zoff is most often associated with Juventus, a club he joined in 1972. His eleven seasons with the Old Lady of Italian football brought him the league six times, the Italian Cup twice and the UEFA Cup in 1977. Zoff retired in 1983 but returned to coach Juve in 1988. Despite victories in the UEFA Cup and the Coppa Italia, he was sacked in 1990. He then spent four years at Lazio where he became club president, a position he held until being approached to manage the national team in 1998 (he guided them to the runners-up spot at

Euro 2000, a match they could have won had France's David Trezeguet not scored a Golden-Goal extra-time winner).

Zoff resigned and returned to Lazio, helping them to third place and qualification for the Champions League in 2000. He then had a brief spell at Fiorentina before stepping down from football at the highest level.

**Name:** Dino Zoff

**Born:** February 28th 1942, Mariano del Friuli, Italy

**Position:** Goalkeeper

**International Career:** 1968 - 1993

**Caps:** 112

**Goals:** 0

**Honours:** European Championship Winner (1968), World Cup Winner (1982)

**The pictures in this book were provided courtesy of the following:**

GETTY IMAGES
101 Bayham Street, London NW1 0AG

WIKICOMMONS
commons.wikimedia.org

Design & Artwork by Scott Giarnese

Published by G2 Entertainment Limited

Publishers: Jules Gammond & Edward Adams

Written by Liam McCann